CHANGE YOUR LIFE

THROUGH *Love*

Light

I had followed many lights . . . will-o'-the-wisps and
    fox-fires,
Restless stars and meteors and phosphorus of desires,
    Lamp in the window, fire on the hill,
    Lights by the sea in the night's chill,
    Stars in the dusk . . . all failed.
    Stars dimmed when dawns paled.
    Oil burned low in the window's lamp.
    Fires quenched in the fog's damp.
    Lights by the sea were masked by cloud.
    Hope entombed in fear's shroud.
        Where could I find the guiding light?
        Not in fires that flamed at night,
        Not in stars of the sky's span,
        Not in lanterns fueled by man.

I was stumbling . . . I was lost
In sorrow's smoking holocaust.
    Perhaps I prayed . . . it might be so . . .
    I heard a voice, "Be still . . . and know."
I stilled my voice, stilled my brain,
Stilled my heart's insistent pain.
I was still as primal night,
Knowing, knowing "There is light."
    In my heart a white glowing
    (light beyond the eyes' knowing)
    Warmed and flamed and brightly spread,
    Lighting up the road ahead;
    Road ahead and every side,
    Radiance intensified.
      Light!
      Light.
I shall never fear the night.

DON BLANDING.

CHANGE YOUR LIFE

THROUGH *Love*

By Stella Terrill Mann

AUTHOR OF *Change Your Life through Prayer*

DODD MEAD & COMPANY · NEW YORK

In memory of my father and mother.

FIFTH PRINTING

PRINTED IN THE UNITED STATES OF AMERICA
BY THE COLONIAL PRESS INC.
Designed by Stefan Salter

CONTENTS

Preface

DEAR READER:

Are you entirely satisfied with your life as it is? Are there changes you'd like to make? Would you change grief to joy, worry and fear to peace of mind and body, failure in any part of your life and affairs to glorious and successful living? And are you soul-sick of a way of life that drenches the world in blood every few years? Do you fear for the future of the human race in this atomic age?

If you are not satisfied with things as they are then this book was written for you. Its purpose is to tell you how to change things by learning spiritual laws and how to work with them. Its special purpose is to show you what love is and how to draw it into your life and how to use it for what it is—the greatest power known to man and the highest of all the spiritual laws.

Please understand that I do not set myself up as a teacher of the spiritual laws, for I know very little. My authority to speak on this subject comes from the fact that my whole life has been changed by *applying* the little I do know. Having caught a glimpse of the Light I yearn to point the way of Light to others. To help to raise the level of the moral consciousness of mankind has become the purpose of my life.

In order to share what I have learned and used in my own life I have for years served as counselor to peo-

1

ple with problems. How we solved those problems by working with spiritual laws has become the subject matter of my lectures and of my published works. This book is the second of a series designed to help others understand and apply the spiritual laws which we have used with such good results.

Lives are changed for the better by learning and using many parts of the Law. For law, as Blackstone said, is a "rule of action." Webster says law is, among other things, the "Will of God, whether expressed in Scripture, implanted in instinct, or deduced by reason." The more we learn and use this law, the more easily does an abundant and joyous life materialize. But all we can hope to do in one book is to stress one tenet of the law so that the reader may better understand how to work with that particular part in his own affairs.

In the first book of this series, *Change Your Life Through Prayer,* my purpose was to define prayer and demonstrate its use in soul growth and the solution of every day problems. It included several case histories of people with whom I had worked in prayer. In that book, we considered Jesus' statement "That if two of you shall agree on earth as touching any thing that they shall ask, it shall be done for them of my Father which is in heaven," and we found it to be pure truth, a part of the total Law, or Will of God. We saw that these words guaranteed the reality of prayer, and we learned how to use that power to solve personal problems.

The casual reader need not go through that first book in order to get the most out of this one. But the serious student intent on changing his life for the better will find it worth while to do so. For prayer, an earnest attempt to communicate with the Infinite Spirit of the Universe which we commonly call God, still is the first step in changing lives and solving problems. It is an instrument to be used with the second step outlined here. Of course the reader may know a great deal more about prayer than the writer. Those who have a method that works should by all means use it! But those who feel they have not been very successful with their prayers will, I believe, find considerable help in that first book.

In all ages and places a few men have recognized spiritual laws and worked with them. But the great *mass* has remained unaware of them. A great many church-going, Bible-reading people of today seem to overlook the hidden or real meaning of some of the most significant of Christ Jesus' teachings. If this fact were not true their lives would be much happier and far more successful than many of them are. This is not criticism. It is an opinion based upon sympathetic observation in working with many such cases. These good people, like Job, have heard of the Law "with the ear," but have not learned how to use it "with the heart."

It is not easy to learn as I early discovered when I first set out to change my own life through prayer and love. I could not see why I had to suffer. Wasn't I a good Christian? Wasn't I a good *Methodist?* "Well then, God, why do you let these things happen to me, if You love me," I cried, as Job had done. But like Job, I lived to learn that ignorance of the law excuses no one. And having learned the law and put it to use, I received from God "more than I had in the beginning."

To discover the laws, the true facts of the universe always has been the most serious work of mankind. This search early branched off into two distinct streams. One we call science and the other philosophy which of course, includes religion. Science has tried to find the "fixed laws." Religion has looked for the "Will of God." The followers of each branch have been pretty sure, and sometimes violently sure, that the other branch was the wrong channel in which to find a better way of life for all men.

Science gives us facts, or knowledge. Religion gives us wisdom. Science tells us how to create the atomic bomb. Religion tells us what we had better do with the bomb once it has been created. Science records all the facts which man has discovered in his physical environment and defines the world in materialistic terms. Religion tells us what is at work in man which drives him to make such an inquiry and declares the real world to be the unseen or spiritual one.

For nearly three hundred years, science has talked people out of their belief in God by presenting a purely materialistic universe. The trouble is, scientists are mere human beings and so make mistakes. That fact should give us no quarrel with science, for it is a search for truth, and therefore prayer. Science makes an earnest attempt to communicate with the Infinite Spirit of the Universe. It asks questions of God and expects answers, though some orthodox scientists shudder at the term and seem to perfer "anti-chance" if they must mention a Cause at all.

Our great Orthodox church leaders are also mere human beings and make mistakes which drive people away from churches and from the knowledge of God. They are sometimes so filled with theology that they have lost their religion. Our churches have become so cluttered with creed, custom, rites, precedent and little church quarrels about the letter of the law that they have quite forgotten or neglected to live the spirit of it. It is an old human failing. Jesus complained about it in His day. But all this gives us no quarrel with the church,

nor with the faithful who hold it together. We still have a duty as individuals to see that our church keeps step with time, and if it does not, then the fault is also ours.

Falling between the apparent contradictions presented by these two branches of the laws, many people lost faith in their old conception of God and found no new one to take its place. So they gave up all religion and suffered accordingly. Their children and grandchildren after them now show the results, among which is our terribly high rate of mental illness. One of the purposes of this book is to aid people in rediscovering God and to rebuild a faith in the help that may be had for the asking.

The long quarrel between our two great branches of learning is coming to a close at last in our day. The wide gulf between them which was but an imaginary one in the first place, is being bridged, thanks to the untiring, honest and often brave efforts on both sides. It is entirely possible that science will yet prove the existence of God and of spiritual laws to a greater number of people than religion has been able to do. At present, religion accepts the existence of God. Its followers have arrived at that conclusion through an inner wisdom and a personal experience which they know in their hearts need not be explained, but which for the sake of others they try to articulate. Science is busy explaining and is coming to the conclusion that God exists. This God is one and the same God. These seekers of truth have been climbing the same mountain from opposite sides. They are now getting near enough to the top to see the same peak. Both sides are now about ready to admit that fact and all the world may well rejoice.

To the reader interested in following this trend toward agreement between science and religion, I strongly recommend the study of two recent books. They are: *Human Destiny*, by the brilliant French Scientist, Lecomte du Noüy, a book that will help you find God and a faith in the future if you have not already found Him, and one that will help you to understand yourself, your fellowmen and all life. Study it. We shall not outgrow it in our lifetime.

The other book is *Man Does Not Stand Alone*, by Cressy Morrison, an American Scientist. His book seeks to prove the existence of God by showing His provisions for man and by presenting living evidence of his theories. No one interested in increasing his faith in God's love and care of man should miss it.

I also recommend reading *Reach of the Mind*, by Dr. J. B. Rhine, director of the Parapsychology Laboratory of Duke University. This book tells about the extrasensory and psychokinesis tests that have been carried on for the past twenty years at the University. Not all who read Rhine's book will accept his findings as proof that man does have the power within himself to influence things to happen in the way he wants them to happen merely by *use of his mind*.

While I accept Dr. Rhine's findings as proof of the existence of certain spiritual laws it is my opinion that not much more progress can be made in this field until the purpose and method are put on a higher level. There is nothing new in these findings, nothing unknown to religion. They are on the right track, for man does have the power within himself to create, to change, to control his world, to get what he desires of life by using his mind in a certain way. *Prayer is a reality.*

The Duke University experiments are of tremendous importance because in them, science is about to say that God could exist even though we are not able to see,

hear, taste, touch or even smell Him. It is about to
admit the possibility that another world other than the
physical, materialistic one exists. Those experiments
are attempts to contact and to work with the forces or
the rules of action; the laws, of the world Jesus Christ
knew so well.

The testers, in trying to prove that the fall of cards
and of dice can be controlled and foretold by *desire*,
are trying to prove the power of prayer whether they
realize it or not. To talk about prayer is to admit the
existence of God. They are working with prayer all
right. But they are overlooking the most important tenet
of that law—*purpose*. The desire is the power, just as
Jesus Christ taught. The word and the thought are
merely used to express, or carry, it. Faith is also a part
of the law. But back of these is the most important element of all, purpose.

To some readers, using a power of the mind, *desire*,
to influence the fall of a card may seem a far cry and
even a sacrilegious one, from using it to predict a harvest months before it is due, or to heal a leper, but to me
the same *power* and *principle*, or law, are involved, the
only real difference being one of *degree* and *purpose*.

Just as we may use the power of electricity to warm a
room or to electrocute a criminal, we may use the law
of *desire* for trivial or for holy purposes. And as we shall
see as we go along with our studies, it makes no difference to the *law of desire* how it is used any more than
it makes any difference to the law of electricity whether
it is used to save a life or to take one. Having free will
and the ability to set this force into motion, man uses
it quite as readily to his harm as he does for his good.
And while it makes no difference to the force itself it
does make a difference to God for what purpose man

uses this force. It makes a difference to man, to—the *difference between life and death.*

The Duke University testers are, whether they realize that fact or not, trying to prove the existence of a law which Jesus stated in the following words:

"Whatsoever things ye desire, when ye pray, believe that ye receive them, and ye shall have them." (*Mark* 11:24)

But Jesus did more than state the law. He repeatedly warned that we dare not set it into motion except for certain purposes within the *law of love,* and He explained what happens when we do set it into motion outside this, the highest law of the universe, the ultimate tenet of God's Will.

The Bible tells us that before we ask, our necessity will be met for it is already revealed. We surely need to know how to use this awe-inspiring power of *creating by desire, asking and belief.* We surely need to know how to handle it far more than we need to know how to handle electricity, for example. Nearly two thousand years ago Jesus Christ met that need by telling us how we must use this law or be destroyed by our own efforts in misusing it.

We have not heeded Christ's warning. And so today there are more people afraid of the future of man than there ever were before at one time in the history of the world. They fear that we have let our machines dominate us; that we lack the necessary moral force (love) to control our material (scientific) creations. Anything, therefore, that science can do to prove that we have this power at our disposal is of tremendous importance for the whole human race. The next step will be to heed the warning about its correct use. We must learn to use it for our good instead of using it for our greed and evil or be destroyed by our own efforts.

Jesus' mission on earth was to show man both how to obtain a more abundant life by learning to use the *spiritual forces* according to their laws or nature, and at the same time, how to use them within the nature of the *highest law,* the law of love. Science has long served mankind in that same capacity by learning the material, or physical laws. But they seem to have entirely overlooked that highest law. Lack of knowledge of the spiritual laws and failure to work within the highest of them, love, has therefore defeated man the world over in his efforts to reap the benefit of the creations of material science. Thus we see ten bushels of wheat grown where two grew before only to be destroyed to sustain prices while half the world goes hungry.

What if the hungry should decide to exterminate those who have wheat? Is there danger of their joining forces with a World Power, which for evil reasons of its own promises to divide the wheat among all the hungry in exchange for armed allegiance? Will the hungry give up freedom for bread, or will they learn how to use their freedom and the spiritual laws at their disposal to provide bread? And who shall teach them—in time? Shall we use atomic power to create a better way of life than any civilization ever has known, or shall we destroy all mankind? How can we be freed from the threats of extermination of the human race?

Jesus announced that if anyone would believe in and apply the truths He taught, those truths would set them free. Truth, says Webster, means "real state of things; fact; reality; a true statement or proposition; an established principle, fixed law." Jesus' whole ministry was one of proving that man has *within himself a power that rightly used will heal, prosper, guide, lead him on to eternal life!* Learning how to use that power should be the biggest business of our lives for when wrongly used it leads to failure, tragedy, sickness, poverty, death and finally, utter destruction.

Merely hearing about the power will not save us or change our lives. Not all who say "Lord, Lord," will be saved, but only those who "doeth the Will of my Father." We must *use* this power, and we must use it in a spiritually legal manner, that is, according to God's highest Will, or within the law of love, all good for all.

No one but a fool or a madman would attempt to work against the highest spiritual law, God's Will, if he understood what he was doing. Once we get a glimpse of this highest law and watch it working inexorably time after time, increased knowledge of the law of love will become the most important thing in our lives. For by right use of it we can obtain the good desires of our heart and by wrong use of it, lose all we have ever held dear, including our own soul.

In the largest sense there are not laws, but a wholeness, God's reality, Law, perfection of Being. Our little finite minds, however, cannot possibly cope with so stupendous a whole. We must break it up into parts and call it the laws, the total of which is the Light.

Catching a glimpse of the Light is, I believe, what happens in all true conversions. The penitent or seeking soul sees a fact, an established principle. Suddenly he understands something beyond a doubt. The great mystics have told us of their experience in catching a gleam of the Light. I do not for a second compare my small findings with their great ones. But I have had enough experience with the "flash of Light," which is

as near as I can come to describing it, to know what the
mystics were talking about and that they reported truly.

The Light can come to anyone. There is no need for
either intercession or guidance. But it comes only to
those who have made preparation to receive it. We cannot learn what we are not prepared to learn. *Desire to
learn is the first necessity.*

When Paul saw the Light he was with others on the
Damascus road who also saw "a light" but were not
blinded. They heard no voice—did not understand. Yet
Paul saw so much and heard so much that it changed his
life completely for he understood. He turned from per-
secuting to loving and leading. He had believed in force
as a power, and the letter of the law. Now he learned
that love is the greatest power in the world, above even,
the power of thought, and that thought and desire until
brought under love are dangerous. When we study his
life we realize Paul was prepared to receive the truth
even though he had been searching for it in the wrong
direction.

A lifetime would not be long enough in which to
examine fully the truth in the teachings of Christ Jesus.
And the most we can do in one book is to take one little
part of one spiritual law and study it in action and try to
apply it in our lives. That is the purpose of this book—
to look at the working of the highest of all the spiritual
laws, the *law of love.* A number of case histories of people with problems that were solved by learning and
using the law are included in the book so that the reader
may see how to use the law in his own life to solve his
own problems.

This book should not leave you where it finds you. Its
purpose is to show you how to change things. If you will
take it up with an air of happy expectancy you will help

to quicken your mind and so, get the greatest possible benefit from it. As you read, listen to your own still small voice. For nothing I have said here is one-half so important nor half so revealing as that which will happen in your own mind if you will invite it and encourage it to happen. There is a part of your consciousness that is connected with the Mind of God. This book can show you nothing new in life or love or the laws. It can only stimulate you, quicken you to remembering something you have known since "before Abraham was," and convince you that you should put that knowledge to work, now.

Although I have worked on this book for several years and discarded several times the amount of material it contains and have completely rewritten it more than twenty times, I still am not satisfied with it and must beg the reader's indulgence with its faults. Perhaps it is impossible to say exactly what one desires to say. But it does give some relief to attempt to say it.

May God bless your reading of these words.

And now come, my brother, my sister, and let us talk about love. Let us first learn what it has done for others, then learn what it really is, how it works and finally, how to use it and to trust it to change our lives from all that we do not like to all that we desire them to be.

Los Angeles
September, 1948.

PART ONE

The Nature of Love
and How It Works

CHAPTER ONE

What Love Can Do for You

You should not waste your time reading a book on how to change your life through love unless you are convinced love actually can do something for you. Your first question should be, "What can love do for *me?*"

The answer is, love can do anything for you that it ever has done for anyone else and more. For you are a unique being. There isn't another one like you in all the world nor shall there be again. Nature never repeats a pattern. She is so prolific, so rich in design and material that she need not repeat ever. But what she has done once she can do again, and better. So, whatever your need may be, whether for persons, conditions, things, principles, place, soul quality or whatever, the fulfillment of that need already exists, and this is true whether of not such a need ever has existed before in the history of the world. You will find the fulfillment of that need and see how to use it, by putting the *force of love* to work in your life.

Here are some examples from life which will give you a hint of what love can do for you.

Love can heal your body.

A young woman learned about love when she woke up one warm Sunday afternoon and found herself lying in a hospital bed. In a moment of clear consciousness between opiates, she discovered she had met with a

15

terrible automobile accident; that a fight was being made
to save her life; that it was thought necessary to amputate her legs; that it had been decided they must operate
by the following morning if they were to save her life.

Touched by the young woman's loneliness and her
apparently tragic unhappiness, one of the nurses, herself the mother of a girl about the age of the patient, said
to her, "My dear, life was not made for sorrow. Life was
made for love and joy and happiness. How does it come
that you, a pretty young woman are here alone, in a big
city hospital, facing death before you ever have lived?
Where is your husband? You have talked about him.
What has happened in your life that makes you so bitter?"

Seeing love, and not idle curiosity in the eyes of the
older woman, the girl began to weep but could not
answer. The nurse went on to say, "I am going off duty
now, going home. If you will give your consent I shall
pray for you this afternoon. Not just for a healing of
your injuries, but for your soul's welfare. I shall pray
for love to come into your life, for all life's sadness turns
to gladness, when love comes in."

The patient wept bitterly, her body shaken by the
sobs of hatred and unhappiness she had so long held in
her heart, and told her story. She hadn't wanted to live.
She had wanted to die. Young and inexperienced, away
from her family, motherless, she had made an impulsive
and very bad marriage. She had "gone through hell with
that beast of a man," she said. On the Saturday morning before, she had gone to talk to her husband's
attorney about a divorce. The unjustness of the husband's accusations further imbittered her soul, set up
such a turmoil in her mind and body that she went
hurtling along the highway in a powerful automobile,

"so mad I could not see, so unhappy I did not care, wishing I could kill N——, determined never to let him have any more of my money, determined never to appear in court and listen to his lies," she confessed.

The story finished the patient said, "Please pray for me. My mother prayed for me when I was a little girl and as long as she lived. But I don't seem to know how—"

That afternoon, drowsy with pain killing drugs, the girl lay silent. Down in the open court yard of the hospi-.tal a little band of Christian workers gathered to sing. They had a tambourine, a guitar and a drum to make music. Up on the warm afternoon air and in at the open window, came the music and the words of love in the form of a song, words that have given courage and direction to millions:

> "At the cross, at the cross,
>   Where I first saw the light,
>   And the burden of my heart rolled away—
>   It was there by faith, I received my sight,
>   And now I am happy all the day!"

"Happy! Happy!" cried the girl in pain. "Oh my God, I must find happiness or die! Give me happiness, God, or let me die."

Her soul sought God, not a doctor, not another pain-killer, not physical aid. When the soul is nailed to a cross of trouble, when the burdens on the heart become too heavy to be borne alone, we always and rightly call on God. And we always are answered.

The girl began to relax as she listened to the singing, the cheerful boom, boom, of the drum. Hope, never dead in any heart, began to stir within her. She began to heal from that hour. A great throbbing, new vibration, the rhythm of love, the desire for a good life had been put into motion within her. And love always heals. All that afternoon the girl lay thinking of her early childhood, of her mother who prayed and sang "those lovely old church hymns as she went about her housework." It was found to be unnecessary to amputate her legs. That afternoon the girl began a search for a better way of life which did not stop in the hospital. Her cry for help was answered. Her words, "I hate you God, I hate your world," changed to words of praise and thanksgiving eventually. She learned that we have a power within ourselves which, if wrongly used, will destroy not only our bodies, but our very souls, yet when rightly used will heal our bodies and lead us on to a glorious life, not only here on earth but through eternity.

Yes, my friend, love can heal *your* body, too!

Love can keep you out of prison!

A man who had been in prison for six years told me that every man there realized the hardest fight he ever would have to make in his life would be that of trying to stay out, once he was released. This is understandable when we consider the fact that most prisoners develop soul-wrecking bitterness, that their prison life and routine kills all natural initiative, robs them almost of the ability to think, so that making a living is in itself a major problem for the ex-prisoner, plus all the handicaps of being known as such. The overwhelming fear of most prisoners is that they will "become repeaters."

This man had left a young wife and a baby son "on the outside." The day he entered prison he told his wife to wait for him, not to divorce him (conviction of a felony being grounds for divorce in that state). He declared that, once out, he would prove he loved her.

"If you had really loved me you wouldn't have gone to prison in the first place," said the young wife who had "been brought up by a religious family that had tried to keep her from marrying me," said the man.

"Her words never left my mind," the man confessed. "For six years I tried to figure out what she meant. I asked other prisoners, the chaplain. I read. Because, you see, I had taken a gun in hand to get things for her. I loved her so much I wanted to give her everything. I thought I had proved I loved her."

The soul's cry to God for Truth, for enlightenment is always answered. That man learned about love. He learned about the kind of love that Jesus Christ said we should have for each other. He came to understand the kind of love Paul was talking about when he said, "Though I give my body to be burned and have not love it profiteth me nothing."

Out of prison, the man continued his studies about love, how it works, how it frees. He put it to work in his life. "And it is the only thing that has kept me out of prison again," he declared. "Half the men I knew in prison have since come out and gone back. Some have gone back three or four times. I have stayed out thirteen years now—every one of them lucky! Before I got out of prison I had learned what my wife meant. I learned that as long as I did not love my fellowmen, as long as I preyed upon them, that I did not love myself, God, or my wife."

What can love do for you? *Love can keep you out of man-made prisons and free you from all the spiritual-made prisons of sickness, poverty, fear and the like*, into which you have, in ignorance or defiance of the law, cast yourself and your mind.

Love can heal your mind and keep you sane!

A woman who twice had been committed to an institution for the mentally ill learned how love can heal the mind and keep one sane. She had been a school teacher but "always had detested her job; never had liked children. For that matter, she had never really loved anyone."

Fearing her mind "was slipping again," she prayed in desperation, prayed earnestly to be saved from another mental breakdown. She was "led to go back to the small town where she had been born and which she had not visited since she had left it years before to attend college." There she spent a summer vacation living in the home of an old lady who was past ninety and had known the teacher's family since before the teacher had been born. In their daily visits the teacher learned about her family history. She learned she had been an unwanted child, treated coldly. "I used to feel so sorry for you when you were a little tyke," said the grandmother. "A child needs love, if it is to grow right. Just as an adult must have love if he is to keep sane."

Those words opened up a whole new world of fact to the teacher, and sent her hunting for other facts. During the summer she learned a great deal about the principle that the purpose of human life is growth toward its ultimate, or God, and that there can be no growth without love, for love is caring which is a mental as well as a spiritual process. She learned that rejecting other human beings, living a life of cold and lonely selfishness, is to cut off the warm mental stimulation which gives zest to living. We do not live by bread alone, but by thought and spirit also, and the ability to think will die out when cut off from the nourishment of love. For love is a two-way force. It must be given as well as received. This sets up a circulation which guarantees mental health.

The wise old grandmother convinced the teacher that "she'd never lose her mind if she could only get enough people to love her, to care about what happened to her." Then to prove she was right, she advised the teacher that the way to get others to love her was to "get real excited about helping others; to take an interest in people." "It will keep your thoughts bright and young," the grandmother declared. And since it had worked for her, one of the most loved figures in the whole community, the teacher decided to try it. For she greatly admired the old lady's keen wit, her clear thinking, the way she kept up with current news, the great joy she derived from other people's happiness, her large number of friends who greatly cared about what happened to their older friend. So, putting the grandmother's advice to work the teacher developed a warm interest in life. She gave and received love, fearing no more the threat of insanity. There was no longer reason to be afraid.

What can love do for you? *It can heal and stimulate your mind, keep it clear and alert, keep you sane and happy and busy and make you feel and act young.*

Love can prosper you!

A business man told me love had saved his business and recreated a fortune for him. "When, after thirty years of hard work, careful building, I faced utter ruin and poverty in old age instead of a comfortable retirement, it was my wife's love and her faith in me that brought me to my senses, stilled my panic, quieted my mind and led me safely out of my difficulties, so that I made a greater fortune than I had before."

The man explained it this way: "I never before had appreciated my wife. I had taken her love for granted. When I began to realize fully what it meant, what she actually had done for me all the years of our marriage, I was shamed to tears. It made me determined to prove my worth, to show her she had not thrown away her devotion, her prayers for my welfare. Somehow, once I got the desire to make a fortune *for her* everything looked different. Before, I was not working for love. I was trying to prove to myself how smart I was and getting fun out of outwitting other business men for my own good. When I began to work for love and with love, to use this power for what it is, I began to prosper as never before. And all fear of ever losing it again, disappeared."

What can love do for you? *It can show you a way to prosperity that you may never have dreamed of before.* For there is money in love.

Love can overcome your fears!

A man came to me for help saying he did not know just what was wrong, but he seemed to fail in everything he tried to do. His parents had been wealthy, and he had inherited a considerable amount of money. But everything he had tried, had failed, and now he was almost broke, he said. His wife was leaving him "because he was such a jellyfish failure."

In the final analysis his trouble was found to be fear. The heart of the law of creation is the phrase "after its kind." Like Job, all that he had feared had come upon him. It was found his fears had begun in early childhood, instilled first by a very austere father who seemed never to show love for his son nor for any other member of his family. In childhood the man had patterned his idea of God after his father and did not love Him nor think

himself worthy of love in return; God and father were
only to be obeyed and feared. Fear had further been
drilled into him by his ambitious mother who always
talked about her son's friends "catering to him not because they liked him but because of his social and
financial position," which made him think of himself
as unloved and unlovable. So he grew up trusting no
one, fearing all for their ulterior motives. He heard more
fear talk from his Aunt, the poor relative who lived with
them and was always fearing the family would "lose
everything." So he learned to fear God, man, the future
and his own abilities.

The man set to work to change his life through accepting love of God as a guarantee against failure in life.
It took several years' work. Rebuilding habits of mind
and restoring the soul is not accomplished overnight.
Eventually the man did learn to love life, to "run and
meet it," instead of trying to dodge it. He built a new
life by learning a new way to live—the way of love. He
rebuilt his fortune. He even got a better wife than the
one who had divorced him because she was sure he was
only a jellyfish and not a man.

What can love do for you? *Love can overcome every
fear you've ever known, every fear you'll ever discover
or build up in your own mind in this world and
all worlds to come.* Perfect love always casts out fear.

Love can build your character!

A man whose goods go around the world, blessing
millions, told me what love had done for him. When he
was a little boy, living on a farm, he came under the
influence and began to adopt the ways of an older boy
who had moved into the neighborhood. One hot summer afternoon he listened to the older boy and ran away
from his chores to go swimming. When he returned in

the cool of the evening his father met him and said, "Did you have a good time, son?"

"I looked at my father's tired, sweaty but kindly face. I remembered the work I had left undone," said the boy, grown to man, "and I began to bawl."

"What are you crying for, son?" asked the understanding father.

"Because you didn't whip me," said the boy. "I know Billy's father is going to whale him half to death; he said so. But you—"

"You are crying because you are a good boy," said the father. "You are ashamed of what you did. Son, remember this day as long as you live. This is the way our Father, God, feels about us. He loves us dearly. He wants us to love Him enough to do the right thing without being watched and forced. But when we fail, our Father does not punish us. We just punish ourselves, son. I make many mistakes in life such as you've made in running away this afternoon. But God does not stop loving me, and I haven't stopped loving you. Why should I beat you, son? You're my *child*. I *love* you. Of course it would please me a heap if you always tried to do the right thing because you'll always be happier yourself if you do."

"But Billy's father—"

"Maybe," said the understanding man, "it is because he does not know as much about the love of God as I do. If he did, he would not punish his son. He would try to instruct him."

That man said he never had found a single problem in his life after that day whether in business, personal or social life to which that lesson did not apply. "I had only to remember my heavenly Father's love, to ask His guidance in any new venture, to ask His forgiveness in

every mistake. I never went into a business deal without
first going down on my knees to ask my Father what to
do and again, to thank Him for the success I knew would
be mine. My neighbor, Billy, was eventually hanged.
He never learned about the love of God, poor soul."

What can love do for *your* child? It can build character into him. It can give his body health, his mind peace
and his heart great joy of living. *Love can direct his life
into channels of good and successful living.* Oh yes, it
can do all that for you, too.

Love can lead you to love!

A tall, gaunt woman, homely by all beauty parlor
standards and no longer young, decided to make a good
and love-filled marriage for herself. Her mother, a long-
time invalid had died and finally she "was free to start
to live some for herself." Long and patient years of
looking after the selfish, ungrateful and dictatorial old
mother had "taught her so many lessons in love that she
felt she could use the power now for her own happiness."

She said, "So many years had gone by that I couldn't
hope to start in and rear a family of my own. So I decided to ask God to direct me to a ready-made family,
a man alone with children who needed all the love I
had to give him and them and who would have as much
love as I wanted to give me in return." That is precisely
what happened.

Is it so strange? If a male mosquito can hear the "love
call" of a female mosquito and by it be directed to her,
what is to prevent one human being, the highest form of
life on earth, from "tuning in" to the vibrations of a
desire to love and be loved by another human being and
from being directed to that other one by some manner
much too subtle for the physical senses to detect or the
human mind to understand? I am sure it not only can

be done but is being done every day in the week. People leave their homes and meet love, the perfect life-partner half-way around the world. When the lover says "Where have you been all my life? I have always been looking for you," he is more than likely stating a simple truth whether he knows it or not, for love always leads to love.

The more determined the desire for love the more surely will it lead on to love. For the desire sets a force into motion which cannot refuse to act when the law of its nature is complied with any more than our electric light globe can refuse to let the electric current flow through when all the rules of the law of electricity have been complied with.

What can love do for you? Why, *it can lead you to love, to more joy in living than you ever have dreamed possible!* Of course, it must be love and not some other force which you set into motion if love is what you desire.

Love can teach you the meaning of life!

"When I received word that my only son had been killed in Germany during World War Two," said a gray-haired man, "I felt defeated by life. I was angry with God for letting this happen to me. For weeks I cried out again and again 'If God exists why does He permit wars that kill our sons?' Then one night I got my answer. It came to my mind as clearly as the tones of a bell. 'You yourself helped to kill your son.' The accusation staggered me because I instantly saw that it was true. I was in World War One. Fought in Germany. I knew war was hell. But I had done nothing in all the years after to prevent war. I had done nothing to make the world a better place for other men's sons. I had not even prayed about it. I had thought I was doing my whole duty to my son by working hard and saving money for his college education. I thought that proved my love for him. Now I know the difference. I no longer blame God. I ask God and the Soul of my son to forgive me and I know I am forgiven, for I am making amends as best I can with the life and love I have left. Now I really understand the meaning of life."

"When I think upon the mystery of life, the possibilities of man, and the glory of growth, I am overcome with love for my Creator," said a devout man. "Every doubt of the future leaves my mind, and my soul knows peace regardless of what turmoil is going on all around me in the world outside."

"When I look at my child and realize there is a bond of love between us, a communication beyond all words, I realize this must be God at work in my child and in me, and I tremble with love of life, with gratitude for being, with thanksgiving for the glory of love and of life," said a young mother. "Then I realize I do not need to worry about my child's future. God loves him too."

"I love a good fight," said a man engaged in fighting an evil in his city that corrupted youth, threatened the whole town.

"I love my work," said a woman engaged in helping others find happiness and a good way of life after she had lost her son and her husband and seemed to have nothing left to love or live for.

The artist loves beauty and seeks to produce and reproduce it with form, line and color. The scientist loves facts and spends his lifetime seeking them out. The American Constitution was framed by our forefathers' love of freedom and their heart's desire to guarantee such freedom for all their countrymen. Lincoln loved liberty and justice, placing such a high value upon them that he declared "no man is good enough to own an other," and helped to abolish slavery. Albert Schweitzer felt his white brothers over the world had so illy used their black brothers that some compensation should be made to them. Consequently, he gave up a great career in Europe to help the black men of Africa, and all the world of justice and good has loved him ever since. Spinoza loved truth so much that he braved the anger, the very ex-communication of his fellow Jews, in order to stand by his principles, and all the world of justice and good has since cherished his memory for his stand.

Does love always win? Is love wholly good? What about the following:

A young woman who "loved excitement, loved a good time," shot and killed her mother who attempted to keep her from going out one night.

"I love my people so much," said a young man, "that I would gladly enslave the rest of the human race and make them our servants. Anything less than such love is disloyalty."

"You are supermen; you alone are fit people to rule the world," said the German War Lords to their followers who loved their children, their way of life above all other children and all other ways of life.

"I loved her so much I couldn't bear for another man to look at her," said a man who had murdered his wife.

"I love my dogs more than I ever could love any human being," said a woman taken to court because her barking dogs had disturbed a fatally ill neighbor; dogs that had repeatedly ruined her neighbor's gardens.

"Love me, and the world is mine," wrote the poet.

"I love you!" Around the world those are the dearest and most longed for words in all the human language. Even the babe at his mother's breast knows the value of love and lets the fact that he wants to be loved known to all. In turn he knows whether he is loved or rejected. And all his life long, he will continue to listen for those three wonderful, thrilling words, "I love you!" For without love there is no living, but only a frustrated and unhappy existence in which one might as well be a turnip or a turtle. We never outgrow the need for love. The old, at death's door, look for signs of love in the faces about them, listen for it with the inner ear as though hoping to hear the voice of God saying, "I love you."

Why do we so desire love, need it, die for lack of it? When we have the answer to that we shall be in possession of the secret of life itself. Is it possible to find the answer? I think so. I have found an answer that satisfies me. Part of the purpose of this book is to share the answer I have found.

If the reader will make sure he has grasped the principles set forth in the next chapter before he goes on with the book he will have no trouble understanding the case histories which follow after that, nor will he have any trouble in applying those principles to his own life and affairs.

We have found the answer to our first question. We have seen what love can do for us by seeing something of what it has done for others. But the answer raises other questions. What happens if we do not choose love? How shall we know whether it is the kind of love that leads to prison or the kind of love that prospers, heals, frees and inspires?

We shall find the answer to those questions by learning *what love is and how it works.* So far we have only looked at the results where love has been at work. Now let's talk about love itself, what it is and what it is not.

CHAPTER TWO

We Must Love or Suffer

WE ARE setting out on a life-changing project. The more
clearly we understand exactly what we are attempting
to do the nearer shall we come to doing it easily and
well. The first thing we must do is to learn about the
nature of this force which we hope to use to change our
lives for the better. Most of us think we already know
all about love, but if we did our lives would be very
different from what they are. So, to begin with, let's
consider the *need to know the law, or rules of action of
this force called love.*

On every hand we recognize the necessity of understanding the nature of the law, or rules of action,
governing forces all around us. For example, we know
better than to pick up live coals with our bare hands.
We observe that there is a physical law which says fire
burns. We respect that law. We understand its rules of
action. We know it will not respect us. We know it so
well that we teach our children at a very early age to be
careful how they handle fire for fire will not be careful
of them. Yet fire is a friend of man. There could have
been no civilization without it. Only a stupid man curses
the fire which he has allowed to burn him. A wise man
learns how to *use* fire within the rules of its own nature
and so he makes of it a servant and a blessing.

Again, when our airplanes do not fly we do not sit

down and cry that God is against us. We remember the force of gravitation. We look to the laws involved in aeronautics. We try to conform more nearly with the nature or rules of action of the forces we are trying to use. And if our electric light globe burns out we do not sit in the dark and sigh that because it is the will of God, we should suffer the darkness with humility and grace. No, we look to the *law of the force* called electricity and meet its rules of action. Yet when we find ourselves in prisons of fear, pain, poverty and shame we seldom stop to realize that we must have been breaking a spiritual law, or failing to work with the nature of one we have set into motion to get the end we desired. We seldom see that now, we are paying the penalty, or experiencing the result.

No, we don't stop to consider that fact. Yet that is exactly what happens whether or not we know anything about the force or the law of its nature which we have set into motion and whether or not we were trying to break a law. While we speak of breaking a spiritual law we cannot actually do so.

How long it will take the human race to learn as much about the spiritual forces and the laws which govern them as it now knows about the physical ones, no one can say. But the real world is the spiritual one. The spiritual laws are above the physical and mental laws, which Jesus taught and proved, for example, when He walked on the water.

We are constantly setting the spiritual forces into action. For example, every time we think, hope, plan, fear, desire, speak, act, or in any other way use our free will, we are dealing with the spiritual force of creating. Right use of this force creates a blessing; wrong use creates a harm, even unto death. Throughout the universe the rule holds true. The force will serve us or master us with equal ease whether we are working on the physical, mental or spiritual plane. The choice is up to the user, always.

Obviously, we cannot live long enough to learn the nature or law of all the spiritual forces. But there is one way to be very sure we are using them to our good and not to our harm, and that is *to learn the nature of the law of the highest force, love, and then to live within that law.* That is exactly what we have already agreed we are going to do.

We are now ready to ask: *What is love* and *how does it work?*

Webster defines love as "the benevolence attributed to God as being like a father's affection for his children; also, men's adoration of God in gratitude or devotion."

Jesus said, "God is love." He then defined God as Spirit. The Spirit of a thing is the essence or reality, the intent or purpose of it. So God is the very Spirit, or intent of love. Then love must be pure goodness. Love is also creative power, the very Father on whom Jesus called to do the mighty works we today call the miracles. Therefore love is the power which created both man and the universe, the power which also sustains them and carries man forward. Love is a force which creates progressive good. Since good means beneficial and since the crux of the law of creation are the words "after it's kind," then love is a force which creates good and good only.

If love is a power which creates only good then it must be an intelligent power able to select, reject and sustain. It must be able to decide and to remember. Thus we see that it is impossible for us to define the terms of love without defining at the same time, the nature, or rules of action, of this force—how it works. Jesus' life and teachings throw more light on the subject of the nature of love. He said, "If ye love me keep my commandments" and also, "Feed my sheep." He loved and so He fed the multitude, healed the sick and raised the dead. Love always acts. It is a dynamic, not a static power.

But we need not look outside our own hearts to know that if we love we want to do something about it. And the more we love the more we want to do. We know that the evolution of man on earth (his true progress from the animal toward the Divine nature) has been the result of love, the desire for good, at work. This is true whether we are talking about God at work for man, or man at work for God or man at work to promote the welfare of his child, himself or his neighbor. All recorded history proves this fact. For example, all we know of justice and freedom for the individual, courts, laws, protection of human life and property, is evidence of *love at work*. If it is love, it gets things done, always.

Love always desires and works earnestly to promote the welfare of persons or principles. It gave America freedom of speech, press, peaceful assembly and religious worship. It also gave us votes for women, child-labor laws, public schools and is trying now to eliminate race barriers. We see love at work all around us. Its nature and its purpose are to give, serve, unlimit, unbind, free, build, empower, beautify and harmonize. It takes pleasure in serving, appreciates, makes glad and forgives. It is grateful, blesses and is a blessing. In the final analysis, it will be found there can be no created good without love. Without desire for good, all actions are idle or evil and end in results which will eventually have to be torn down. This is a fact which the psalmist made clear in the words, "Except the Lord build the house, they labour in vain that build it." The Lord is the principle of love which created the universe and maintains it. Everything contrary to that Spirit will eventually fall, just as the idea of Divine Right of Kings, witch burning and slavery have fallen.

Throughout the ages the moving, liberating power of love has been observed by all men, consciously used for definite ends of good and growth by a few men, but misunderstood and wrongly used or left unused entirely by most men. Some day we shall use this power as universally as we now use fire. We shall learn then to work with nature at the source. All our present failures in personal and national life can be traced to attempts to work against nature in one way or another.

We could spend the rest of our lives talking about love and never say the final word. We can sum it up by saying *God* is love at work and *Love* is *God* at work. When we set this force into motion for good and holy purposes we cannot hope too much nor dare too much. For *when we are working with love we are working with God.* We can word a working definition:

Love is the fervent desire for the progressive good of and the earnest effort to promote the welfare of—.

But whom shall we love? Whose progressive good are we to desire and to work earnestly to promote? What principles or things shall we care about with all the fervor of our hearts and seek to promote in order to change our lives to all good? Jesus summed it all up in the two great commandments as follows:

"Thou shalt love the Lord thy God with all thy heart and with all thy soul and with all thy mind. This is the first and great commandment. And the second is like unto it, Thou shalt love thy neighbor as thyself. On these two commandments hang all the law and the prophets." (*Matthew* 22:36-40)

We do not get the full significance of the fact that all the spiritual laws hang on, or derive from, the commandments of love until we consider all else that Jesus taught. We are too likely to think of them as a beautiful ideal, something to think about on Sunday, a conception of a way of life impossible to man, designed for angels only. This reasoning leads us to thinking that the law remains merely an ideal, and so, has no teeth in it. A study of all the laws Jesus taught, indeed, our own observation of life all around us, our recorded history, analysis of our own problems, bring us to the realization that we *must love* or perish as individuals and as the human race. There is no way out.

Yes, we must obey those commandments in full, or perish. Such obedience is not merely a form of worship and cannot be done by lip service alone. It is a necessary part of life. It is the truth, an established principle of existence. It is the way things are. We must set the spiritual forces into motion according to the dictates of all good, love, or be destroyed by these same forces. Such destruction is not a punishment by God. It is self-destruction in spite of all God's laws of life which would save us forever, if we would but obey them.

Love or perish is a spiritual law far more exacting than the physical law which says eat, take nourishment or starve to death. For there is a way of obeying the higher, or spiritual law that makes the lower or physical one null and void. This is a truth which was demonstrated many times by Jesus. For example, He "had meat to eat" which His disciples knew nothing about and He turned water to wine, when He desired to serve His

friend and host (love at work) by working on the physical plane.

*We must love or perish because we have the power to
harm and to help ourselves. This power is our ability to
create by desire.* Nature, or God, having brought man
as a puppet, an animal pulled by instincts which he could
not disobey, to a certain point of development, gave him
free will which he uses to set the law of creation into
motion. In this he has the same power which God used
to produce both man and the universe, the power of
creating by the Holy Trinity, the Big Three, which are:
Desire, Action and *Belief.*

Jesus talked about this power throughout His ministry.
He summed it up in the following words: "What things
soever ye desire when ye pray, believe that ye receive
them, and ye shall have them." (*Mark* 11:24)

All we know of life is *desire, action, belief.* Our *desires* include all our hopes, our aims and our plans
whether we ever voice them or not. They include all the
things and conditions we ask for when we pray. And
this is true whether it concerns our desires for ourselves
or another. Our desires may be good or evil, voiced or
held in silence.

Our *acts* include every thought we think, every word
we speak and every deed we do. They include our prayers and our curses, our praises and our blames, our
thoughts of poverty and sickness, our compliments or
complaints.

Our *belief* includes all we accept as true, all that we
think of God, man and ourselves whether that which
we think happens to be true or not. It includes our faith
in the foot of a dead rabbit to bring good luck as well
as our belief that our earnest prayers will be answered.
It includes *all our fears.* Fear is a strong belief and sets

forces in motion which create after its kind. For that is
the law of creation whether on the physical, mental or
spiritual plane.

Now when these three, *desire, action* and *belief* syn-
chronize, the creative force then moves on our behalf
according to our word, because the rules of action have
been complied with. And this is true whether we have
consciously used the force or merely blundered into
using it; just as we can deliberately press a light switch
or accidentally fall against it and produce the same result, a lighted room.

All we know of life is *desire, action, belief.* Desire for
good is love at work. When we desire good we are in
tune with the highest power in the universe, we have
listened to our highest or love nature, our Christ self.
Such desires promote our highest welfare. The good in
them is accumulative. But when, through ignorance,
fear or wilful intent, we desire evil (anything against
freedom of growth toward good whether for ourselves
or another) , we have listened to our lowest or lust nature. Such desires hold us back in evolution and head us
into mistakes which do not solve our earthly problems
but increase them. If persisted in after we learn about
the highest or love way, they will destroy us. Our actions
and our belief will fall in line with our desires if those
desires are strong enough. So the key of life is to look to
our *desires.*

The highest law is love, God's Will for the promotion
of the welfare of all men. God is not mocked. We cannot
act against that law of good and growth for all without
paying the penalty. The nature of the universe is good,
and no one can try to harm it without being hurt.

No one can injure his brother or attempt to enslave
him, to keep him from growing, and achieve final good

from his attempt. But man has kept on trying it ever since Cain slew Abel. The world has just seen a colossal example of the proof that love is the highest law. Hitler used that Holy Trinity, the spiritual force of creation, *desire, action, belief.* But he used it in a spiritually illegal manner, for a spiritually illegal purpose—outside the highest law, love. His desire was for power at any cost. With his scheming, distorted, lustful mind, he believed in men, arms and murder as a way of achieving his desire. His acts, including his thoughts, words and deeds, were in line with his desires and his belief. And surely enough, at the lower level of the law, it worked for him. Being law, it is no respecter of *persons* nor of *purposes.* It could not be and remain law. So it worked, producing "after its kind," until the higher law stepped in as it always does, sooner or later. Love ultimately stops the one who works against good. Thus Jesus says "On these two commandments hang all the law and the prophets." Love always has the last word. For God is love.

The man bent on evil is whipped before he starts. No one can outwit God and overcome the Spirit of all good. We see people who seem to be "getting by" but that is because we cannot see far enough nor deeply enough. We are judging after temporary appearances and not after final facts. The element of time confuses us. It is not so difficult to accept the fact that all wrong doing, all acts against nature or the Will of God must surely be stopped in time or we'd have chaos, not cosmos. We know "order is heaven's first law." It is first law of earth too. Not even the vegetable and animal world could proceed without it. The difficult thing for most of us is to see that we daily punish and limit ourselves by getting out of order, by failing to live within the three parts of the two great commandments.

If we are to change our lives for the better we shall have to understand those commandments. The law of love being threefold, let's take each part separately and see why there is no safe way to use any of the spiritual forces except in obedience to love. This will show us why we must first surrender our hearts to love before we can hope to change our lives and affairs.

First, we must love God with our mind and heart and soul. Why? Because nothing less than such love is perfect love and perfect love alone can *cast out fear*. When we cast out fear we no longer set forces into motion which bring to us the things we fear. And generally speaking it is the things we fear which will hold us back instead of taking us forward. A deep belief in them brings them to us.

The world has too long thought of loving God as a beautiful idea of worship but not a very necessary or practical means of earning bread. Now the truth is, as Jesus taught over and over, that the way to get the material things of life is not piece meal through struggle, but by discovering and using a power within ourselves, by setting into motion a force in which we live and move and have our being; a force which loves us and desires to promote our welfare, but unwilling to usurp our free will, waits for us to call upon it before moving on our behalf. By loving, desiring all good, believing in all good and calling upon this force, we do set it into motion for our welfare.

We live in this Spirit of good, and we have it within us. "I in the Father and the Father in me." Jesus explained the working of this force, love, in the Lord's prayer.

We can make our outer life, the earth, according to our desires even as we can our inner life. We can create a heaven on earth. But until we learn to love all good with our whole *heart,* which means our deepest interest or purpose in life, and our *mind,* which means our active thoughts which dictate our deeds and words, and with our *soul,* our very measure of being, we shall be asking amiss in our prayers and not aright. For we shall be asking in fear or ignorance or evil. We shall be asking, as Jesus said, that we may spend it upon our lusts. And we shall wind up in trouble every time by asking and receiving that which hurts us!

We must love God, the principles of good, truth, justice, mercy, everything that we know to be good, or we cannot really love life. The purpose of human life is growth toward the ultimate, God, or good. We cannot desire to grow toward perfection, to go on in evolution, unless we love life. For we have free will. The choice is ours. No desire, no growth. No growth, and we cease to be, for we cannot stand still and we cannot go backward.

Again, God is pure goodness. If we do not love goodness we are not for it, we do not seek to promote it and will foolishly, like Hitler, though perhaps in a very mild degree, work against the dignity and freedom of the individual and so, wreck our own soul.

We cannot hurt God; cannot stop the law of progressive good for all men. Not to love goodness is to hurt ourselves even unto death. We dare not go against God's Will because to do so is to go *against ourselves.* We dare not remain coldly indifferent, for to do so is to *stop evolving;* to perish. There is then, only one thing to do, exactly what Jesus said, love the Creative Spirit of the Universe, the power of all good which we commonly call God and seek to promote the principles of the good life on earth. Not for God's sake, we must remember, but *for our own!*

That we must love our neighbor as ourselves is the second part of the commandment. Why? Because if we fail to love him we are either hating him or being coldly indifferent to him. If we hate him we set up in him a hatred for ourselves because the doctrine of the law of creation "after its kind" is alive and ever at work. Love and you create love for yourself. Hate and you create hatred for yourself. Furthermore, our hatreds set up poisons within our own body and mind which ruin our health and happiness as doctors and psychologists warn. Hatreds curtail our chances of success and growth and create fears and desires for revenge in our neighbor that will some day have to be reckoned with. Witness the world's race and political problems today.

If we are merely indifferent to our neighbor and fail to love him, which means fail to desire good for him or to work earnestly to promote his welfare, we shall find our own good endangered by his ill. His poverty will eventually tax and rob our property. His groans will disturb our rest. His sickness of mind, body, soul and economy will come to live with us whether we want them or not. They will come through pressure of race beliefs, mass hatreds, evil desires, fears that breed war, ignorance that endangers, aggressions that lead to restrictions of our liberty.

If we do not care enough about our neighbor's welfare to teach and persuade him to a better way of life then his delinquent children will mar our children's future. The cost of the necessary power and laws to restrict him from drunkenness, murder and thievery will rob our purse and blackmail our heart.

There is no way out. *We must love our neighbor for*

our own sake! We must do unto others as we would have them do unto us because our very lives, our daily welfare, our happiness, peace of mind and our eternal life depend upon it. When we love our neighbor we multiply our good beyond computation for to love him is to desire good for him and to work with him and for him. This *desire, action* and *belief* will create "after its kind" and put us in tune with the very purpose of life which is growth for all men toward all good. Loving our neighbor increases our own good ten thousandfold. When we drain his swamps, we rid our own cities of the malaria carrying mosquito. When we help him to a higher standard of living, we create a market for our goods. When he adopts our culture and our ethics, he becomes a delightful friend and companion. Oh yes, as we do unto others we do unto ourselves, and every man on earth is our neighbor. He becomes our brother when he arises to put off his animal lust and accept his higher Christ self, living after the laws of love. And we are not true brothers until we are one in Christ. Then are we the sons of God indeed. Before, we are only the children of God.

Loving our neighbor is not only a form of worshiping God. It is a necessary part of evolution. Eventually we shall rise to the level of moral consciousness which desires the love of all men for the great joy it gives. But until then, the best way to save our own lives and good is to love our neighbor as ourselves.

The third part of the law is that of loving ourselves. Why? Because until we do learn to love ourselves we shall find we cannot really love God or our fellowmen. To fail to love ourselves is in the largest sense, to deny God, to refuse to accept the very gift of Life within us. If we do not love ourselves we will not seek to promote our own welfare. We will sulk and hide and deny our gift. To love ourselves is to stir up the gift of God within us.

Greed, selfishness, cruelty, hatred, laziness and other loveless qualities or acts prove lack of respect and love for self or soul. If we do not love ourselves we shall not desire to reproduce ourselves. We shall not even promote or attempt to maintain our physical and mental health.

If we do love ourselves we make every attempt to continue to live, to love, to learn and to grow toward our ultimate destiny. We should all be happier than any king ever has been! We should be glad that we exist and keenly aware and appreciative of our abilities with eagerness to use them for our own good and for the advancement of all men in God's plan for man. Until we can truly love and appreciate this being which God created and needed, we may remain ethical and be "good" perhaps, but we will merely exist, not live. If we do not love ourselves we may reduce our whole lifetime to little patterns of conduct of which we and perhaps society in general approve, accomplishing little, vegetating, failing to measure up to what the Spirit of Good expects of us.

Summed up, we must learn to obey the commandments of love, or perish. On the other hand, once we learn to bring every *desire, action* and *belief* under the law of love, we shall find the solution to every problem known to man, and we shall grow on, in peace and joy beyond our present ability to imagine, toward perfection, toward God.

There are two sides to love: we *must love* and *we must accept love*. To fail in either is to defeat our own purpose in being on earth.

But how are we to bring every *desire, action* and *belief* under the law of good? First, by establishing love as the highest law of our life. We start this process by surrendering our hearts to love. This will bring our desires and our belief under the law of love. Then we shall learn to speak, look, listen and think with love which will bring all our *actions* under love. When we have gone that far we shall have no trouble in trying to work with love and will trust love to solve all the problems of life.

Strictly speaking there is no separation in these steps to changing our lives through love. We break them up here in order that they may be more easily handled. Their total is our attitude toward life, which includes our attitude toward God and our fellowmen as well as toward ourselves. For life is a wholeness made of many parts.

To review before we start the process of surrendering:

We create the conditions of our lives by our *desires, actions,* and *beliefs.* Our desire tells the creative force what it is we want it to do. Our prayer, or request by word, deed and thought, sets the force into motion to produce that which we have desired. Our faith or belief is our mental acceptance of that which we have desired or ordered. When this has been done the law of creation has been complied with, and it is done unto us.

We are going to learn how to stop desiring, acting on and believing in that which will harm us, substituting all that which will produce good in our lives, the lives of others and the very universe itself. Along with this we are going to learn how to *accept* love. For love is the force which creates good. Its nature is to create more good than existed in the first place. Its purpose is to carry the beloved forever forward.

PART TWO

How to Establish Love as the Highest Law of Your Life

CHAPTER THREE

Surrender Your Heart to Love

HAVING seen what love is and what it can do for us, and having recognized that we must love now or learn by suffering to love eventually if we are not to perish, we have decided, have we not, that we are going to change our lives through love. The question is, how to go about it? What shall we do first in order to start our life-changing project?

Since we cannot change the law of love any more than we can change the other spiritual laws we must learn how to change ourselves by bringing all our desires, acts and beliefs under the law of good for all. In this way we can change not only our daily lives and affairs for the better but our very destiny, as well. Nothing less than good will permit our growth here or hereafter.

The first thing we must do then, is to *surrender our hearts to love.*

To surrender means to "yield to any influence, emotion, etc.," says Webster and further defines heart as "the seat of life or strength; hence mind; soul; spirit." Our purpose then is to place our strength, our life, our mind, our soul and spirit under the influence of the Spirit of Love.

We may hear about the law until doomsday and never once get a benefit from it unless we put it to work. Until such surrender is made no one can do much for the one

47

who would change his life. Even Christ Jesus did not
help before he was asked. Jesus' formula of "Wilt thou?"
and "Dost thou believe?" put the issue squarely up to
the sufferer. Jesus was not a dictator or a fighter. He
was a teacher. He explained and demonstrated the laws.
He forced no one to accept the Spirit of Love as a way of
life. Nor does that Spirit, God, force us. We have free
will.

Since Jesus Christ knew more about how to change
lives than any man who ever lived before or since, we
do well to study His method. Until we rise to that height
of moral consciousness and love which He knew and
felt, we cannot hope to do the works He did. But we
can learn His method and use it at our own present level
of understanding and love. We do not know all that
Jesus knew but we are very sure about two points in His
method of healing for we can so easily prove them in
our own lives. First, we must *believe* we can be helped
and secondly, we must be *willing* to be helped. We have
to fulfill these two requirements before we can hope to
change our lives through prayer and love. Prayer is asking. Love is desiring. Faith is believing.

The more we know about the methods of changing
our lives, and the more we can grasp of the cause and
workings of the spiritual laws, the more quickly, easily
and permanently our change will be made. We can be
certain that Jesus' three words "Dost thou believe?"
referred to His whole teaching and not just the simple
idea that the one asking help had to believe he could
be helped. Somehow, by His great love of humanity
and His perfect understanding of the spiritual laws,
Jesus was able to go directly to the inner perfect soul of
the sufferer and remind him of all those truths of existence which he had known "since before Abraham

was." That is not a strange phenomenon. It is one we use every day. Let's look at it a bit further in order to understand it better so that we too, can use it at will.

First, we know that what is true on one plane of existence is true on all planes. For example, we know that the human body remembers all that it ever learned through the ages of man on earth and uses this stored knowledge any time the need arises. This is true of the mind, too. Psychologists tell us that human experience is never completely wiped out, but is stored in the subconscious mind of the individual so that anyone who understands the laws or rules of action involved can uncover those hidden experiences and bring them up into the conscious mind. Science says these memories of the human race have accumulated for millions of years.

Now if mental and physical experiences are never lost but only filed away safely until needed and called for by the *individual,* it necessarily follows, does it not, that all spiritual experiences, facts and rules are also remembered. They too are stored, ready to be called upon at any time when needed *by the individual.*

What is true on the physical and mental plane of existence is also true on the spiritual plane. This is exactly what Jesus taught and proved. The trouble is, we don't yet know how to dig into our own souls and uncover these memories of spiritual experiences, rules, forces and actions in the way that Jesus knew. To know how to do this is the missing link between our being able to do what Jesus did and our desire to do it.

We should not leave this one point before we are thoroughly convinced that there *is* a way for the individual to get in touch with his inner spirit or soul, a way to remember the law and learn its use. This is the Father within, through whom we must go to the Father without, God. This is the Father within, through whom Jesus called to the Father without. It explains what Jesus meant in saying "I in the Father and the Father in me."

An example of the way this works on a lower level is known to all of us from the experience of parents with their children. A child starts to do something he should not do, and at one look or word from his parent, he stops. The parent does not have to go through all his teaching, all the do's and don't's back to the child's infancy. He has only to *remind* him with one meaningful glance, one firm word. That one glance or word stirs the child's life-time of memories, and he then acts accordingly. Whether he obeys or attempts to disobey is purely a matter of free will.

So with us all, our Father is the God of the Universe. *We know* His rules and the results of breaking or abiding by them. The missing link is the *need to be reminded* for we are still children in this matter. Jesus reminded the penitent of his real self, his true worth, of the laws, of his right to be helped, of the advantages in correcting his life. At the same time He reminded the sufferer that he had the privilege of refusing, that he could go on in his own way if he desired. He reminded him that he had brought his troubles upon himself and that the trouble would reappear if he continued in making the same mistakes.   •

We can sum up Jesus' teaching and all else we know of spiritual laws in the same way Jesus did, by asking ourselves three questions:

Do we really believe in good as the highest way of life?

Do we honestly, earnestly desire to change our lives?

Do we honestly believe there is help for the accepting?

If so, then let's actually surrender our hearts to love. The reader will want to find his own way of doing this, but for the assistance it might give others, I present here the method I use when people come to me for help. I suggest that they first get their mind and spirit into the state of receiving and of love. I have found it helps to study the Bible, especially the book of St. John, and also the twenty-third psalm, the ninety-first psalm and Paul's words on love in the first Corinthians, the thirteenth chapter. It is up to the one who desires to surrender his heart to prepare himself with such thoughts and feelings as will help him in his purpose. But having arrived at that place, I suggest he then silently read through the following questions and answers, then go back, silently read the questions again and make his answers aloud.

1. Do you believe in the existence of a power higher than the power of the mind of mortal man?

Answer, *I do.*

2. Do you believe this power is all good, all mighty, all seeing, all knowing, all loving and that its purpose of existence is to produce good in the universe, in all men?

Answer, *I do.*

3. Do you believe this power which we commonly call God, created man and so, must have his best interest, his highest welfare, at heart?

Answer, *I do.*

4. Do you believe in the power of prayer, the ability of man to communicate with this great infinite spirit of the universe and by such communication to receive help and guidance in all affairs? At the same time, do you believe in the ability of this Spirit to receive the thanks and gratitude and love of man?

Answer, *I do.*

5. Do you believe that you have the free-will choice of working for God's plan for the freedom, eternal growth, the final perfection of all men, or of refusing to do so?

Answer, *I do.*

6. Do you believe in the eternal justice and fairness of the laws of God, all good, which hold no man finally responsible until he understands the law and then, knowingly chooses against it?

Answer, *I do.*

7. Do you understand the nature of this law of love which produces only good, to be unbreakable, unchangeable, above all the other spiritual laws?

Answer, *I do.*

8. Do you see that ignorance of this law and attempts to avoid or contradict it, whether wilful or unintentional, must necessarily bring an unhappy result in the life of anyone?

Answer, *I do.*

9. Do you believe in the mercy, the kindness and justice of this law which forgives man his mistakes as often as he calls upon it for forgiveness, provided he is truly penitent and earnestly intends to mend his ways?

Answer, *I do.*

10. Will you try to do your part honestly, cheerfully and in all faith that your whole life and all your affairs may be changed for the better?

Answer, *I will.*

11. Will you honestly try to avoid all spiritually illegal desires, actions and beliefs hereafter?

Answer, *I will.*

12. Once your life has been changed through love and prayer and all good is working in your own heart, mind, body, and affairs, will you do your part to teach, inspire

and help all men to this way of life by means of love rather than by force?

Answer, *I will.*

If you can answer all the above in the affirmative you are truly ready to surrender your heart to love. Now go to your closet, or meditation room. Close the door to shut out all disturbances. This is an outer symbol of going in secret to the Father within. If you cannot get down on your knees in an attitude of surrender, then stand and lean your arms on the wall for support, resting your head on them with your eyes closed. Give yourself up to a definite feeling of *letting go* your old way of life. Release all feelings of unhappiness, hatred, desire for unfairness, all fears concerning your own welfare, all doubts about God's ability and intention to restore you. Surrender to a definite feeling of willingness that God should come into your heart and mind to make of you a center of love and to rule over your life from here on.

Say in effect:

"I believe in God, the Creative Spirit of the Universe which created me and gave me free will. I believe the Spirit is all good and that it has the power to heal, to prosper, comfort and guide me in this world and in all worlds to come. I now surrender my own will and my way of life to this guidance of God, pure good, and I do so in faith and in happiness."

Pause, wait awhile. Then assume the feeling that the conscious, hearing, feeling, knowing Spirit of Love has been contacted and that it offers to come into your life to guide your every desire, action and belief, to heal you of the result of all past mistakes, to accept your wish for forgiveness, to wipe away your tears and heal you of all sense of guilt and shame. Consciously accept that offering, saying in effect:

"I receive the Spirit of Love. It is now established in me. There is no doubt about it, no argument about it. It is so. I shall now be helped by the power of love. I shall work with the law of love and trust the spirit of love. All my desires, actions and beliefs are now under the guidance of all good. I am blessed and I am a blessing. And I am grateful that this is so."

Having announced your intention to make of yourself a center of love which both receives and sends forth love, the next step is actually to put these good resolutions into effect.

Love always desires, works for and believes in a better way of life, a more abundant life, a perfect life for the object of its affections. You will now desire and start to work toward a better way of life for yourself and in accordance with God's plan for man.

You will start to work with the divine principles of truth, honesty, justice, mercy, fairness and all the qualities known to be good. You will want to enjoy more liberty and freedom in your own life and at the same time help to work for it in the lives of others. All your prayers will include the words "in perfect ways of love."

You are starting out now to live an abundant life of all good. Love is the highest synonym we have for good and for God. Therefore, when we believe in a better way of life, we have *become aware of God*. When we see a better way of life for ourselves and all men, we have learned to *listen* to God. When we start to act on our new belief and vision, we have started to *work* with God.

But how are we to do all that? By daily, hourly, striving to bring every desire, action and belief under the law of good. This, in turn, must be done by learning how to look with the eyes of love, how to speak, listen and think with love.

With all our theories down on paper, let us now see how they are actually put to work in life. Let's look at the rules in action.

The reader seriously interested in changing his life should at this point start his notes and affirmations. First, decide what it is you most of all desire to change. Give it a topic. Write it down. Now write:

I believe in the power of love to change my life from what it is to all I desire it to be. *I believe love can* . . . . (heal, bring me peace of mind, prosper me, whatever it is you have written down above) *and I ask it to do so for me.* I am eager and willing to do my part. I thank thee, Father, for the joy and privilege of working with thee, in Love.

CHAPTER FOUR

Look with the Eyes of Love

Now let me tell you about Jenny, who appeared to be one of the most hopeless cases that ever came to my attention. But her purpose was one of love. Her problems covered all the points we shall be discussing in the chapters that follow. The significant ones are italicized for the reader's later study. If the reader will compare these points with those of his own problem, he will likely find where he has been making mistakes and how to rectify them, thus making his demonstration complete.

In reporting Jenny's story, events seem to move swiftly. Actually, they covered a period of more than five years. The one who desires to change his life should not be impatient if those changes do not become immediately evident.

When people come to me for help, I require of them a very full history of their lives which must include their early childhood, list their hopes, fears, desires, successes, failures and state as nearly as possible what they believe their present trouble to be. The history includes facts about their formal school, religious training and what life itself has taught them. The purpose of the history is to get an accurate estimate of their *total attitude toward life* which will include their attitude or deepest feelings about God, man and themselves. This explains their *desires, actions* and *faith,* shows where they have been making mistakes, and is a guide to what must be corrected.

These case histories cover about forty pages of typed business letter sheets. Some of the most revealing facts in them are not the points which they play up but the ones they try to hide. *Shame is a belief of being unworthy* of God or man or both whether there is any real cause for such feeling or not. Shame always proves a lack of both self-respect and self-love.

When the subject cannot get his story onto paper, he comes for conferences instead. Jenny "talked it out." Her formal education had stopped in the fifth grade. Her story soon revealed that pain, grief, poverty, shame, frustration, fear and worry had taught her many things about life not found in school books and much of it that was not true. But *the things she believed had come upon her and had been done to her.* Jenny started earning her living when she was thirteen, and since she was sixteen had done so mostly by "being a bad woman," she told me naively.

Jenny's first words to me were "Some said you wouldn't talk to me if you learned I was a bad woman, but *I knowed you would.*"

This proved her *unbounded faith* that *help could be had* regardless of her past or present state. Her faith had *set into motion* a series of circumstances which finally had deposited her at my door. Her *desire,* her *actions* and her *belief* had synchronized on that one point.

When I asked Jenny if she could state her desire in one sentence she said "Yes'um, I can. I want to learn how to be good," her bright blue eyes glowing with hope and determination, "so's I can teach my granddaughter,

Nellie, so's she won't turn out bad like me and her mother did."

Jenny was an illegitimate child. Her only child, Violet, was illegitimate. And that daughter's only child, baby Nellie, was illegitimate. Jenny was thirty-seven years old and Nellie was nearly a year old.

Jenny's childhood history was one of work, pain, and strife to learn, of being unloved by her mother, unwanted, kicked around from pillar to post, sick and often hungry. Her early girlhood was a search for love, protection and beauty, resulting only in the lust, desecration, and filth that she *feared* and *believed* she would find for they were all she knew, all she had seen of life. Later she got it into these words for herself, "I was associating with animals not men and women." The crisis in her life which brought her to me was occasioned by Violet's running away, leaving the baby with Jenny, and blaming her mother for all the troubles in her own life.

When we are hurt badly enough we take steps to do something about it because the soul knows the purpose of human life is growth toward an abundance on earth and eternal life. The soul always warns the outer, mortal man of danger. If the outer, mortal man heeds that warning, he moves toward safety. The Prodigal decides to return to his Father, the giver of abundant life.

Jenny was determined to "give the baby the best of everything," but she did not ask for "an awful lot of money" to make amends to that baby and to her daughter Violet. She wanted "only enough." Jenny did not ask for a rich couple to adopt the baby; did not ask how to be freed from her duty. She actually was not asking anything for herself except where those two she desired greatly to help were concerned. She had become so determined to help them that she had actually begun to do so. To put faith and love to work for a purpose of love is to be able to call on the Creative Spirit of the Universe for help and to get it.

In order to demonstrate a part of the Spiritual laws governing love on which anyone may call for salvation when his purpose is one of love, let me tell you how Jenny actually came to her decision to seek help. Having reached the very depths of despair after Violet had fled, reviling and repudiating her, Jenny saw no way out of "her messy life." But she confessed a fact which long had been trying to gain admittance to her consciousness: *she was somehow at fault.* The Prodigal must confess before he can be helped.

Jenny decided the best thing she could do would be to drown herself and the little granddaughter. She was willing to take her life so that she would no longer be an evil influence to her daughter by "setting a bad example." She was willing to take the baby's life because she felt no hope for the child and "thought it best for it to die young, while it was innocent and before it had suffered." Her willingness was an impulse of love to right a wrong she had done. But her solution (drowning) was not one of love but one of fear and confusion, a decision of her own free mind, the mind which so often makes mistakes.

Jesus taught that the spirit outweighed the matter or the letter. *Jenny's spirit, her real intent was good.* Her actual desire was to help. So she dutifully went down to the river and sat there trying to think it all through clearly to be *"sure she was doing the right thing, for once, and wished somebody would tell her what really was right to do."* She had lost faith in her free-will way of life and was unconsciously seeking God's guidance.

Suddenly Jenny began to think about two people in her town whom she knew and admired. One was a young man, a doctor, the other a middle-aged woman, a school principal. Jenny admired them because "They were good and helped people." The heart that loves good is on the road to a good life regardless of present and temporary appearances because it is the hidden spirit, or intent that counts. Jenny was *unconsciously desiring to work with God*. But she did not know how.

An airplane droned high in the blue June sky overhead. Jenny looked up. It "popped into her head," that there was a "way to learn how to live life like the Doctor and Principal lived, just like there was a way to learn how to pilot a plane." And Jenny instantly *decided that she could and would learn*. Decision is the first step in any demonstration; the first step in prayer.

There is a spiritual law which says that the answer to our problem already exists long before we realize we have a problem. Our job is to call. Jenny had called. And she got her answer, too. For she "began to realize it would be wrong to drown herself and the baby." So she got up and went home "already feeling better," and dimly aware that "something already had changed." Soon after, she ran across some of my published articles which "gave her courage to pull up stakes and come out to Californy" (half across the continent!) to ask my help. The reader should note that everything that happened to Jenny afterwards was a direct result of her *desire* at work. This desire was *spiritually legal*. There remained for her *acts* and her *faith* also to fall within the law of love.

From the first, Jenny realized that money alone would not solve her problems. "I worked for some rich people," she said, "and they ain't no better than an'body and just as unhappy." It was one of those same rich men who had "got her into trouble the first time when she was only sixteen and right pretty." Unconsciously, Jenny was just as afraid of money as she was of men and all life because her only contacts with men, money and life had been unhappy ones.

Jenny was very sure about what she wanted to do for Nellie. She had a *definite purpose*. She didn't want Nellie ever to be hurt by life, and she didn't want Nellie ever to hurt anyone else. She was very *sure it would not be necessary to hurt others in order to help Nellie*. Thus, you see, she was bringing her desire and belief under love even though she did not know that fact. Part of her plan for achieving her goal was to "straighten herself up so's I won't be a disgrace to Nellie."

More than she knew how to express, Jenny wanted to be freed from her sense of guilt and shame. For when she began to think about how she had failed in life she sometimes "had to get drunk and forget it all to kind of rest her mind for a spell," she explained. Then when she sobered up, she admittedly would "hate herself for wallowing like a pig."

This cycle of spiritually illegal acts, constituting an attempt to run from the Lord, had repeated itself until Jenny had "come to the end of her rope" when Violet left her. Then Jenny had, unknowingly, surrendered her heart to love. She had decided there was a better way of life than the way she had been living and was desperately trying to find out how to live it in order "to be good." Jenny's was the *first move* in changing her life. By taking the initiative she had *opened the way for help*. I cannot speak for other teachers but as for myself, I never work with a student who has not already come to the point of free-will surrender. As I understand the laws, I have no moral right to try otherwise. To do so would be, to my mind, an attempt to coerce, or usurp the free will of another. But Jenny came to me ready to go to work to change her life.

At first she wanted to run, to "get away from men and mess and everything," in order to study, to learn a new way of life. She thought she would make great progress if only she could get a quiet little home in the country, a little chicken farm, she suggested, and "be away from everybody."

"No," I said, "you do not need seclusion. You need action. We cannot run from problems. We must stand in order to conquer. You cannot change your life by sitting at home meditating and repeating affirmations. You must *do* things, live the affirmations. You have taken the first step, surrendering your desire to love, now you must follow up with *actions*."

But Jenny was afraid that as soon as she "met new friends out here it would be just like back yonder, in trouble again."

With Jenny, I always had to illustrate the principle before she could grasp it and start to make use of it. Jenny owned a little old green rattle trap car which she called the Green Turtle—because it moved so slowly. I used it as an example many times to give her a picture of a principle at work. I said "Jenny, how did you learn to drive the Green Turtle, by taking care of chickens in the country or by getting into the car and *trying to drive?*"

So eager was Jenny to change her life that her mind was constantly stimulated beyond her normal ability to understand. She sometimes amazed me by the quickness with which she grasped an entirely new idea or principle I was trying to explain to her.

"You mean," she said, "that in the law of love I'll have an accident if I don't learn to drive straight, not to cut the button, stay in my own traffic lane, park right and watch out for the cop in case I forget and accidentally break the law?"

"Exactly," I said. "The difference is there is *no way* to outwit the keeper of the laws of love. They need no policeman, no courts, no judge. The instant you break a part of that law the penalty starts taking toll at once in your life and affairs."

Jenny had had considerable first hand experience with policemen and the man-made laws. The man Violet had run away with was an ex-convict. Jenny thought heavily for a while and then said "Are you sure there ain't *no* way out?"

"No way out," I repeated. "You can no more break the law of love and get by with it than you can keep the sun from rising."

"Then what have I got to do?" Jenny asked, ready to listen, ready to try to obey for she had accepted as truth beyond dispute, that there is no way to break the law of love.

I then explained to Jenny the nature of the law of love about as I described it in the previous chapters, stressing again and again that it is the highest law and that not even our prayers are of any avail to us unless they come within that law.

Jenny knew there were such things as a city ordinance, a county, a State and a Federal law. Soon she understood the law of love in relation to the other spiritual forces at her disposal and expressed it thus: "Like a Federal law is higher than the little laws of our town and we can't make a little law contrary to that higher one."

After much discussion on all points before mentioned,

Jenny said, "When you told me I had to change my whole life you shore hit the nail on the head. Reckon my own daughter won't know me if she ever does come back."

"Never say *if*," I warned. "Say *when*." Jenny had already seen that she must bring all desires and all acts under the law of love, all good. Now she had to start to bring all beliefs under that law, also.

Jenny's four steps in seeing, speaking, hearing and thinking with love composed her actions. These four, of course, occurred simultaneously, although I have separated them here for the sake of clarity. To show Jenny how to look with the eyes of love I used a picture phrase which proved so helpful that I repeat it now.

When Jenny drove she always wore green colored sun glasses. I said, "Jenny, when you wear those glasses everything appears to be green even though you know the clouds are still white and your dress is still gray. As soon as you remove the glasses which give a false color to everything then you see things in their true colors. Your first step in changing all your acts to love is to take off your dark glasses. They color the world with hate, fear, signs of failure, poverty, suspicion, jealousy. Take them off and *see things as they are*."

"I get it," said Jenny. "Green means ignorant too. I got to wise up and stop being a green horn."

When Jenny had that picture straight I added: "This means you must learn to see all things, God, your fellow-men, and yourself as *good*. And you must see this regardless of outward appearances. For the *inner spirit is good*. It is by seeing this good in ourselves and in others that we help to bring it forth, to develop it in ourselves and in others. In that way we are loving and serving God, ourselves and our fellowmen. We are then

working with the Spirit of all good. We also must see
the value of good principles. We must practice and up-
hold all good such as truth, honesty, decency, justice
and the like."

Jenny had a deep respect for, or perhaps a fear of, the
law. And she wanted to learn to "keep all the law." But
she did not see how she could love herself or see herself
as good. Wasn't it enough if she just loved Nellie and
her daughter? But I explained she had no choice if she
hoped to change her life. "To love yourself is one third
of the great command. You cannot wait until you have
cleaned up your life before you love yourself. It works
the other way. You must *love yourself* in order to overcome shame, defeat, fear, bad habits, all the unlovable
qualities. You have to think too well of yourself to permit yourself to indulge in such habits, for only then can
you break them. There is another side to it too. If you
do not love yourself others will not love you. If you
think ill of yourself you will be projecting this idea to
the world around you and it will continue to respond to
you according to those ideas. You *must see yourself as
good!*"

"But how can I?" Jenny groaned. "Just look at me!"

I led her to a large mirror and said, "Look at yourself
and tell me what you think the world sees in you as you
pass by."

Jenny stared long and honestly and said, "They see
a big bulgy woman more than a hundred pounds over-
weight, wearing a size forty-eight dress so tight it looks
like the skin on a sausage—" She began to weep and
could not go on.

I took it up and added, "With blonde stringy hair
long unloved and neglected. Suspicious eyes, a sour
mouth, cigarette stained fingers, run over shoe heels."

I did not spare her. Rather, I accented her faults including a whining voice in order to rouse her to decision and action. I included all her listed aches and pains. When I had done laying on with a trowel, I said "Jenny, we are three-in-one. We are what the *world sees,* and judges after appearances. We are *what we see as we'd like to be* but have not yet become. We are what *God sees* which is our highest Christ self; that is the *reality.* Now, close your eyes and tell me what you see about yourself that you'd like to be."

Jenny straightened a little and said she saw "a woman who had reduced, cleaned herself up, learned how to be good and who had stopped making a fool of herself."

"Now tell me what you think God sees in you, Jenny."

But Jenny knew little about God. She never had gone to Sunday school in her life. She had "sneaked in" to church a few times "mostly for the music which was so pretty" and because she "liked to be near good, clean people."

Jenny's heart was seeking harmony, perfection, and paradise. Her Christ mind, the Father within, never had lost sight of God, the Spirit of all goodness, the Father without. This is true of all men regardless of their present level of moral consciousness.

Jenny thought God was a "big old man sitting in a golden chair up in heaven." She thought "If he likes you He gives you a break. If you're bad and He catches you at it, He sometimes smacks you down unless you beg Him not to."

In conferences that followed I was able to tell her in a way she could understand that to the Great Infinite Spirit of the Universe, which we commonly call God, she was a pure spirit and so without sin or shame; that the moral free mind and human flesh could and did make mistakes but that the pure spirit being spirit is not subject to the laws of flesh. Jenny understood pretty well from the first that the purpose of life on earth was to try to make our every day outer life like that inner perfect Christ model. "Like kids trying to learn in school," said Jenny.

But at that moment standing before the mirror I said, "Now look again while I look at you. What I see in you is the real and eternal. I do not wear colored glasses. What you see in the mirror is the false, unreal, the temporary. You are looking through dark glasses."

Jenny's big body stiffened. She stared hard at the mirror as I said: "I see a happy, charming, attractive woman who has come out of the prison house of flesh and pain and mistakes; who walks the paths of peace; whose joy has been made full. I see a woman who is honest in heart, clean in mind and body, true in spirit; a woman who has found love, who looks, speaks, listens and thinks with love; who works with and trusts love. I see a woman who cannot fail, a woman God loves and trusts."

Jenny let out her breath and was silent a long minute. Then she looked me squarely in the eyes and said, "You ain't lyin' to me. And you couldn't be that mistaken. So if you say you see it then it's true. Tell me what is the first thing I got to do to make it so clear I can see it too!"

"You already have done the first thing," I said. "You *desired* to change and you *decided* to do so. You must continue to try to *act, think, speak* in line with that desire. Along with it you must have faith, must *believe that it will come to be as you desire.*"

For months we got no further than talking about the law of love, desiring all good, working for all good, every hour of our lives. In the simplest words I could find, I told Jenny the story of man on earth, his search for Truth, God, and his findings of the law, order and beauty of the universe. I recounted how God had implanted within every man the desire for eternal life, perfect unending liberty. As Jenny listened to me she was sure she could put the law of love into effect and satisfy all her God-given urges within the law of love. But when she was away from me she "met up with people who had no idee" of the law and no intention of living within it. She would come in half angry, very much puzzled and to her everlasting credit, would pick up my Bible and demand, "Tell me what it says here about this," relating some experience she had had.

I encouraged Jenny to continue thinking about God as a kind of understanding and all wise Father which is what Jesus recommended that we do. She never tired hearing the story of Jesus. One day when I was reading to her the account of our Lord's crucifixion and came to the world's outstanding prayer of love, His prayer, "Father forgive them for they know not what they do," Jenny burst into tears and said, "While that dirty howling mob wanted to hurt Him more!" Then getting hold of her emotion, she added, "He did that for me. But what can I ever do for Him that will be big enough to pay Him back? You say He came to show us a way of life that will save us all if we will follow it. What can *I* do?" This was gratitude at work, a form of love, and from that hour, I knew Jenny never would give up trying "to be good."

As we went on with our studies Jenny often sat in silent awe as I explained the meaning of our lessons. By an instinct, a teaching from within far more instructive than anything I had said or could say, Jenny began to see something of the reality, the power of love. She began to desire good for herself and for all the world as well as for Nellie and Violet. She began to see because she had set her heart on love. Jenny's Christ mind was speaking to her outer, free mind. I had only to stimulate her to the point of inwardly listening, *reminding* her. Any time we really listen, we shall hear the voice of good, God. Just as any time we really look for it, we can see good all around us. Jenny had begun to look with the eyes of love.

Jenny never tired hearing about Saint Paul. I never tired telling her, never tired reading to her Paul's words on love as given in the thirteenth chapter of *First Corinthians*. There are no other words in print which so exactly and so beautifully set forth the properties and the responsibilities of love. Once when I had read the entire chapter to her, Jenny sat gazing into space as though listening to far-off music. Then she quoted some of the words that had made the deepest impression upon her mind: "Suffereth long—is kind—endureth all things —is not easily provoked—thinketh no evil—rejoiceth with truth—hopeth all things."

"And believeth all things," I reminded her.

"I guess," said Jenny, looking as though she had come to a tremendous decision, "I guess I ain't learned nothing yet. I guess that's the kind of love I got to try to have. I see now that everything I've ever done in my life is wrong. I got to learn to look differently. I see now what you mean by false green glasses. I got to learn to look at Harry differently too, and at Tilly—" Jenny had quite a list of people who had "done her dirt" whom she had hated and reviled for years never once aware of what these emotions were doing to her own mind, body and soul.

"The problem is to *see everything and everybody as*

good in spirit," I reminded again and again, "and then to help that good to come forth, being sure you let good work through yourself at all times."

"But how can I be sure whether it is my bad self or my good self at work?" Jenny wanted to know.

"By asking yourself about it. Is it a good and growing thing? Does it have hate, bitterness, criticism in it? Does it help you or anyone else to grow nearer to good? Does it carry you forward, leave you standing still, or turn you backward in your search for good? Is it a belief in limitation, a silly habit, an idle word, an abusive word that helps no one, or is it a growing good word that helps all?"

Jenny took a package of cigarettes from her purse and placed it on my desk and said, "Must I stop smoking too?"

"What do you think?" I asked. "Does it lead you forward? Does it make your plans for Nellie come closer? Does it make you conscious of God or is it only a time-wasting habit behind which you hide from other duties? Can you afford to burn up your money when you need so many things for Nellie and yourself?" Not long after Jenny had given up smoking entirely which I considered a tremendous victory for her. She already had given up drinking. I once told her life was too short to spend any hour of it with a muddled mind. "You are throwing away the greatest gift God ever gave man, the ability to think, when you deliberately cloud your mind, temporarily render yourself incapable of clear thought, disconnect yourself from the God mind, the source of all creative power." When Jenny finally understood it, she stopped drinking. To prove she did understand she said, "When I'm drunk I can't hear God talking to me."

Slowly, slowly, Jenny began to look upon the world as one of *goodness*, friendliness and love where it was entirely possible to find peace, plenty and harmony. Since her only means of earning an honest living was her ability to "cook up a mess of vittles," she went to work in a small restaurant where she had ample opportunity to practice her newly acquired rules of life. She no longer shied away from meeting people. "It's the kind of joint I need to work in," said Jenny gratefully. "Everything there is wrong. I'll get in a lot of licks at trying to hold my temper, trying to look, speak and listen with love."

Each time she came for help Jenny would go to the mirror, stand there, child-like, and say, "Please tell me again what you see in me so's I can *get the picture* in my mind to last me all week while I'm sweating in the kitchen. I want Violet to see me that way when she comes home." Jenny had long since stopped saying "if" about the things she desired. And she was learning to visualize her desires as an aid to bringing them into manifestation.

Slowly, painfully, Jenny kept at her task of trying to "keep her mind out of the way and let Christ's Spirit work through her." She tried to look at her fellowmen, the world around her and at herself as she imagined Christ Jesus would look and see. Slowly her *desires*, *acts* and *beliefs* began to mesh. By her very singleness of purpose she began to change and to see change in herself and in the world around her.

Jenny was making progress with her program but she still was "hating that man Harry," who had run away with Violet. So one day I told her to stand before the mirror and said "Now, think about Harry. Think about how you'd like to break his neck." That was her most often repeated phrase about the man, and it was always spoken with a great deal of bitterness.

Jenny did as instructed and watched her face become tense, her mouth tighten, her eyes harden, her whole body react to the thought and feeling "I hate." She then followed instructions and stood thinking about her little granddaughter and let her eyes say "I love baby Nellie and I am going to do everything I can to promote her welfare."

Jenny was finally convinced that we do not look with our eyes only. We look with our mind, our feelings, and our faith as well as with every muscle of our body. For what our eyes see our brain reflects throughout the entire body. To look with hate, fear or doubt is to put a mark, invisible at first, very evident in time, upon the entire body, mind and affairs. Our total attitude toward all life grows out of the way we look at religion, or our deepest belief about life.

"I have been my own worst enemy," said Jenny, ready at last to stop blaming the world. She had a great talent for love, and she had been using it against herself. She had gone out of her way to take people into her home to help them. But they had "always double crossed her just as she had seen they would." She had *expected the worst* even while she had repeatedly hoped for the best. The strongest feeling is the one that wins because it is the one we have the most faith in. It will dictate our words and acts. All her life Jenny had *believed in bad luck* and had *looked for trouble.*

Along with Jenny's efforts to speak, think and listen with love, she was trying to trust love and work with love. She was trying especially to trust love in regard to her absent daughter from whom she had not heard since she ran away. In this she did what I always recommend when trying to help a loved one; she placed a circle of love around her. This is a process that will not be considered in Jenny's story which we are to conclude in the next chapter, but it will be fully discussed in chapter ten with a life example of how to help a loved one.

Before we go on with Jenny's story let us pause here and check up on your own problems and your desire to change your life for the better.

Stand before your mirror. Do you like what you see? Look around you at your home, your surroundings, your city, out into the world. Are you satisfied with things as they are? How do they affect you? Do they stir you up to help, build, comfort, and encourage or do they only irritate you, arouse your fears, your dislikes and even hatreds? Be honest with yourself. Are you looking at yourself, life, your fellowmen with eyes of love? Are you looking for trouble? Do you see things as limited and hopeless, all bad, all good, or inwardly good with room for improvement on the outside?

Tomorrow when your new day begins start to look with eyes of love. See good everywhere. See others as Christ Jesus would see them. Let your eyes tell others you trust them, have faith in their inner spirit of goodness. Let your eyes look past their outer mistakes straight to their inner Christ self. Look with sympathy. Look with admiration. Look with hope. Look with eyes that understand and forgive. Look upon the news of the day not as all fearful but as all that is good. Let others know you see good in the world.

When you first waken in the morning say, "Today I shall look with the eyes of love and love will look back at me."

For your notes: Make a list of all your faults which

you see, which you realize others must surely see and which you believe God must see. Then make a list of all your good points, your desires, acts and beliefs. List your good habits and intentions. Now subtract the bad from the good and see what your score is. Then write a new list. Write down the things, qualities, etc., you are striving to acquire and become, much as Jenny did. Set a goal. Go back to your original note made at the end of chapter three. See whether or not it covers the things you really desire to do. If not, then this is the time to enlarge your program. Set a new goal. Liberate yourself. Then start looking at yourself as I looked at Jenny, as the accomplished, desired self, and not the self which the world sees when you pass by.

Reading every chapter in this book will not help you nearly as much as actually trying to put even one rule into effect in your life.

Now is the time to begin!

CHAPTER FIVE

Speak and Listen with Love

ALONG with learning to look with the eyes of love at herself, her fellowmen and the very nature of the Universe or God, seeing all to be good in spirit, Jenny had to learn day by day to *speak* and *listen with love.* The purpose of all this was two-fold. First, to help her to become aware of a power greater than man and circumstance, a power able to create all good in her life, a power which she must work with hourly, trusting it to lead her forever forward. Second, to help her remember that she must be willing to work with it, that she must first give in order to receive.

From Paul's words on love I typed the following for Jenny:

"Though I speak with the tongue of men and of angels but have not love, I am become a sounding brass, or a clanging cymbal." (*First Corinthians* 13:1) On the same sheet I also typed "He that is of God heareth God's word." (Jesus in *St. John* 8:47)

Jenny was to read these two quotations the first thing in the morning and the last thing at night. Seeing the importance of learning to speak with love, Jenny wanted a "real stiff rule laid down" which she could remember quickly while working. So I told her to remember "Nothing less than love gives you a right to open your mouth to speak."

75

How many millions of needless, time-wasting, tinkling and tinsel words of idle chatter, ruinous critical words of harsh and brassy gossip, clanging cymbal words of confusion and destruction would be saved daily if enough people tried to follow that rule. *Speak with love or remain silent!*

If we want to be coldly calculating about this and say we don't care what happens to other people and their lives but we do want to change our own for the better, we still have to learn to speak with love. For there is a spiritual law involved in the matter. "Every idle word that men shall speak they shall give account thereof in the day of judgment. For by thy words shalt thou be justified and by thy words shalt thou be condemned." (Jesus in *Matthew* 12:36-37)

We have no choice. Our words do become flesh and dwell among us as horrible or as helpful, as building or as destructive as enriching or as impoverishing as *we ourselves make them.* "After its kind" declares the unbreakable law of creation. And every day is judgment day. Once we set a creative force into motion only love itself, the highest law, can hold back the result and make void the lower law. For the lower law, unstopped will, must, create after its kind. Nothing under that law, our tears, fears, regrets, can prevent it. The provision "After its kind" applies to thoughts, things, feelings, words and deeds as it does to trees, animals and men.

People grow discontent, complain that God does not hear their prayers or does not love them enough to answer while all the time the trouble is they neither know how to ask aright, nor how to listen when the answer does come. Paul is right about it. No matter how intelligent we may be, no matter how convincingly we may "speak with the tongue of men and of angels," our prayers avail us nothing if they are outside the law of love. Though we may "have the gift of prophecy, and understand all mysteries and all knowledge" and though our faith could remove mountains, we still are nothing, without love.

There are two parts to listening with love. One is that in truly doing so, we need nothing except that which falls within the law of love as given in the two great commandments. For listening means accepting also. Jenny's "stiff rule" for listening was "turn a deaf ear to everything but good and growth." This eliminates listening to negative or evil gossip, to ideas of fear, words of hate, plans of deceit, limitation and the like. No one should listen to such things for to do so is to turn away from nature as it is, the inner spirit of love which is in everything.

The other part of listening with love is that by our own intent to do so we open the way for all things of love not only to speak to us but also to listen to us in return. We open the perfect prayer channel of communicating with God when we learn to listen and to speak with love.

Daily, hourly, we must live within the law of desire for all, acts that promote the welfare of all, faith that holds to a belief in good. We must speak of love and with love to our fellowmen. We must speak words that build, restore, heal, free. We must speak words that praise, bless and encourage. We must voice our trust, our desire to promote the welfare of all good for all men including ourselves. We should never speak ill of ourselves. If the ill exists, cure it. But to speak of it and do nothing about it is to work a double harm against ourselves.

All the above I went over again and again with Jenny.

I then wrote down some daily rules which worked so well for her that I give them here.

1. Try never to speak when you are angry.

2. Try never to speak when you feel bitterly critical.

3. Never speak of your fears, ill health, bad luck, hard times or regrets of any kind. Work to eliminate them, yes. But negative words and ideas show lack of faith in God to supply the desire for good, and lack of gratitude for the good we do have.

On the positive side I gave the following rules:

1. Be quick and sincere with compliments, looking for honest opportunities to express them. Be generous with praise and gratitude. Speak of the hopeful and encouraging things of life.

2. Speak in tones of happiness, warmth, fearlessness, contentedness and good cheer. Not to be of good cheer is to doubt the goodness of God.

4. At least a hundred times a day say "I thank God for His love and guidance. I thank God for my great good fortune."

Jenny was to let the tone of her voice always indicate the fact that she was happy to meet and to serve others; that she truly liked to listen to them and that she expected to hear something good by listening. At the same time she was to let her eyes also carry a friendly message of warmth and welcome.

Soon Jenny had it all down to a few words and gestures. "You're wonderful," she'd say with her eyes, her voice, her whole manner. "Tell me about yourself!" she'd say and make it sound as if she had said "your very wonderful and interesting self." It was not an act. A new world had opened up to Jenny; a world of honest, friendly, kind and decent people. A world without fear; a world of loveliness. Jenny found the world which she never had known before but always had wanted in her heart. All who came in contact with her soon realized that her gratitude was natural and deep.

We all come to earth with a talent, a special ability which we can put to work to help the world, receiving in return all that we desire of life. For life is fair, just beyond our present feeble powers to understand. No one is bankrupt. Jenny's talent was a natural interest in people. But she had not known how to use it. She had been born for love and laughter. So far her talent had done nothing but get her into trouble.

Soon Jenny had overcome one of her most debasing habits, that of cursing and swearing. "A cuss word just comes so easy," she apologized when I frequently took her to task about it, pointing out that swearing was not speaking with love. Jenny knew so many vivid and descriptive words that she could talk at length without repeating any of them, a fact of which she once was proud. At the least touch of anger she would be off in a streak of sizzling insults designed to burn her victim to a crisp. But as she began to learn that what she really did was to burn herself to a crisp instead, she "held her tongue," when she couldn't actually speak with love. She also had to break herself of her long-time habit of idle gossip with someone she liked about someone she didn't like. "You are talking about yourself," I would tell her. Jenny liked people, and she wanted them to like her. Once she learned what was back of her gossiping she was able to stop it. "Got to stop letting my mouth run," she would say.

Jenny fried hamburgers, dished up French fried potatoes, poured sticky pink dressing over half a head of lettuce and sang out to the waitress who had called her a "big fat cow" to "come and get it dearie." All

the time, she was silently blessing, loving, seeing, thinking, of that girl's highest self. Each day as she worked
Jenny thought about love. She memorized Paul's words
and called them her "beautiful poem that had a tune to
it like a song."

As her sense of frustration was checked, Jenny began
to see real progress for she had at last begun to *love herself.* This was not vanity. Far from it. It was *soul pride,*
more than self-respect, born of gratitude for life. She
had begun to stir up the gift of God within herself. She
no longer drank cups of "coffee-flavored cream, stiff with
sugar," as she once had. She no longer felt the need of
"eating a snack just for company with herself," before
going to bed because now she never "was lonely for she
knew God was always with her." The glare of suspicion left her eyes. A frank and friendly look came in,
a trusting appraisal and approval of others. Her voice
lost its whine and found a new calm, cheerful tone.
Her temper slowly cooled. The day she reported to me
that she had lost a total of "twenty whole pounds of
ugly fat," I knew Jenny would make real progress. For
nothing encourages us in our efforts to promote our
welfare so much as a glimpse of real success.

No, it was not always easy. There were setbacks. For
example, Jenny found it hard to trust an invisible law
to bring her daughter home to her. But she worked and
prayed, succeeded and failed, and started all over again
trying to live a life of good. Once she lost her temper and
threw a heavy iron skillet at her boss. Afterwards, she
got down on her knees to thank God that her aim had
been bad and she had missed him. But in spite of all
temporary setbacks Jenny forged ahead. She *never once
lost sight of her purpose.* She never once changed her desire "to learn how to be good."

From Paul's "love never faileth: but whether there be prophecies they shall fail," Jenny made up a phrase "love never lets you down no matter what anybody says," which she used on herself and others. She had seen it at work before her very eyes on the waitress, Effie, who had called her a fat cow. Effie, who hated the world, herself and her work became Jenny's best friend and listened to her teachings. For Jenny took great pains to find the girl's good points, to speak, to listen to her with love.

Jenny proved good for her Boss' business. He took her from the kitchen and put her out front. Soon his business increased. Help stayed longer than his help had ever stayed before. Jenny became the center around which the whole restaurant revolved. But the man would not increase her pay. Jenny managed not to "hate him once, remembering love will never let me down." She blessed him and continued to look to the Spirit of Love (God) for increase in supply. The Spirit of Love as a power, a guard, and a keeper of books in the world became very real to Jenny.

Jenny's appearance improved. A dentist replaced two teeth which were conspicuously missing, and her smile became charming. Care brought back the copper lights to her hair. She continued to reduce her weight. She stopped "cutting her own throat with sharp words and gossip about others."

Jenny's employer sold his business. She had been telling all who would listen that she'd love to open a roadside stand of her own "just to be sure the public got real good coffee." A customer who had watched Jenny work trusted her in financing her little business. He was annoyed, he said, with Jenny's employer for not giving her a share of the profits she had earned for him. He had "greatly admired her spirit." So once again

Jenny had seen the law work out in her own life and affairs. As she had done unto others it was now being done unto her. Love always keeps the accounts square, just as Jenny had seen and worded it. "After its kind," said Jenny, starry eyed, when we talked it over. "As long as I work for all good I'll never be cheated," she declared.

Jenny's little business was a success from the first. She catered to stray tourists and to the regular truck trade. I went out to watch her in action several times, just to see love at work.

"You're looking fine, Bill," Jenny would say and mean it. Bill would stir his coffee slowly in order to hold back time for Jenny was making time at her place so very pleasant. Bill's heart was just as hungry for love as the heart of everyone else. Have you ever heard of anyone who had too much love? Bill had a wife, a job, a measure of happiness. But not more than he could hold. As with Bill, so with all.

No wonder Jenny's trade flourished. Those tired drivers, half bent to the shape of the cab of their big pounding trucks tarried, talked, relaxed and were warmed by this woman's honest interest, reluctant to leave that interest because it was honest. In all their run no one else made them feel so important, so welcome, so happy as did Jenny. For once her fears were removed, once she had stopped expecting "the worst" of men, she found them to be delightful, interesting friends, who were worth her time and her efforts on their behalf.

Jenny prospered in purse for her friends told their friends to be sure to stop at Jenny's place. Jenny thought "the nicest men in the country came to trade with her." She was aware that the law "after its kind" was still "on the job working for her." Some of those men called her Mom. Some called her Jen. Some just said "Hey, you!" But to a man they saw Jenny's high regard for them, felt her love of goodness, and they liked it, for it spoke to their very secret hearts. Not one of them would conduct himself below Jenny's high regard. They tried to outdo each other in *living up to what Jenny thought of them.* It is the way of life. It is the way of love. It is the method God uses to take the human race forward.

Then one day Jenny said she thought she ought to get married "because it looks so respectable like. I ought to have a man around time Nellie starts to school and a married name to sign her report cards."

"Yes," I agreed, "marriage is the most respectable and the most protective institution ever worked out for the benefit of the human race. But there is more to getting married than just getting your name changed. You must get the right kind of man. You will first have to be the kind of person you want your husband to be. So decide. What kind of man do you want?"

Jenny was very much to the point. "One I ain't ashamed of when I measure his corn by my bushel," she said. "He's got to measure up to my new way of life and love."

We set to work with the *law of attraction* for a husband for Jenny. This is part of the law of love or desire, and it is unfailing. From the first, Jenny *accepted* (through faith at work) the fact that the right man was looking for her; that she would have as much to offer him as he would have to offer her; that it "would be fair." In her usual way Jenny summed it up in a few words. "I don't want a Christmas tree ornament husband. I want a real one. Because I aim to be a real wife and not an imitation."

Eventually a fine looking business man appeared and became acquainted with Jenny's warm smile, her happy outlook on life and her love of humanity. Being a very lonely man he tarried to drink more coffee than he wanted while Jenny's bright and genuine interest warmed his heart. When he asked for a package of cigarettes Jenny said no, she didn't handle them and she didn't sell beer either because she would not be a party to such lifetime wasting habits. "And it sort of stopped him in his tracks and he took a real good look at me," Jenny later reported.

Came the day when Jenny was sure William was going to ask her to marry him. She rushed for advice and to voice her fears.

"I ain't aimin' to marry a man who can't believe as I do, all these things I been learning about God and love and the spiritual laws. They mean more to me than even William does."

"Jenny, Jenny," I scolded gently. "All your life you've wanted love, craved love. You've never before found a man you respected enough to marry. It was this desire, a good in itself, misunderstood and wrongly used which has lead you into most of your past troubles. From all you've told me about him, this William is the man for you, found by the very Spirit of Love and brought by the law of love to you. Now why do you begin to fear when trusting the law has brought you so far on your way?"

"It's his religion," said Jenny. She sighed and looked very sad. "Says he never misses a meeting, goes every week when he's home."

"What is his religion?" I finally broke in.

"He's an Optimist," she replied, looking very puzzled.

"I don't know what they believe in. But if he can't—"

So I told her about the International Optimist Club and watched the quick tears gather in her grateful eyes.

"Oh," she cried slowly, wonder and awe in her voice and face, "the law has worked again! You said I had first to be the kind of person I wanted my husband to be. Well, I mean, ain't I an Optimist already?"

I am sure the world will agree with me that Jenny was an optimist of the highest order.

With the question of difference in religions out of Jenny's mind she turned to her next fear—her past. Should she tell William all? Would love see her through on that? Would the law hold?

"Does William think he is better than Jesus Christ?" I asked. "If so, you'd better not marry him. But if he realizes he is not better than our Lord then I'd say that you can teach him something about love. If he does not forgive your past how can he expect his sins to be forgiven? Tell him to read *John* 8:1-11 (woman, caught in the very act) and tell him that God asks us to forgive our brother seventy times seven if necessary and that we are not so perfect as God, therefore, God surely forgives us more than we can possibly ask. If God forgives you then William must also, or suffer. It is the way of love, and it will see you through. Trust it."

Jenny was silent a while and then said, "For quite a spell now I ain't felt so guilty about my past. Seems like God has forgiven me fully. Every time I look at somebody with love, forgive them their own past sins and shortcomings, seems like my past looks lighter. In my tithing, working for others, I feel I ain't giving away at all, but getting something wonderful instead. I know God is better than anything we can think of. The Spirit of everything is good. It is the way we handle things that makes them bad. But God made them good to begin with."

Thus Jenny had taken another step all by herself. She had learned to *think with the mind of love,* to tune in to the very vibrations of universal good. Fortunate, wonderful Jenny! Most people live all their lives and never discover the fact that this is a friendly universe, that God is indeed the Spirit of Love and everything made by that spirit is good—very good.

Then one day Jenny brought her new husband, William, to tell me goodbye. They were soon to go back to the State from which they both had come and there they would "make a proper home for Nellie," who was ready to enter school. William got me aside long enough to say "I know I'm not good enough for Jenny, but I am going to be as good to her and for her as I can be. She deserves the best. Always doing good for others." He spoke of her many good qualities, her courage, honesty, cheerfulness, her cooking. Everything about Jenny was about perfect, said William. "And," he concluded, "she has the kindest eyes that I ever have seen in a woman's face. Kindest and *loveliest,*" he added, warmly.

Jenny also had something to say to me, in private. She led me to the mirror to which I first had led her more than five years before. "Now I'm going to tell you what the world sees when I pass by," said Jenny. She looked long and earnestly and then said, "They see a youngish looking woman in a size thirty-eight tailored blue suit that is a knock-out for style and beauty. They see a woman who looks washed and clean and who knows what to do with her hair and her hat." She studied herself critically awhile longer, broke into a warm smile and added, "And I guess if they've really got eyes in their heads they see me as the happiest woman in the world."

"Now tell me what God sees in you, Jenny," I requested.

"God sees a woman who is never going to stop trying to learn, praying, being grateful, trying to be better," said Jenny, and I knew she meant it.

Then she wanted to know what I saw in her.

"I see all that you see and more," I said. "I see a child of God, born anew, begotten of God through love, a woman who has established love as the highest law of her life. I see in you a desire to live forever within the law of all good. I see in you a Soul triumphant, Jenny, accepting good as the only reality in the universe, loving God and forever beloved by Him. I see you therefore successful, handling every problem that may ever come to you."

Yes, it was a radiant and confident Jenny who called on me that day. But a few weeks later Jenny came back, white faced, but calm. She didn't need to tell me —Violet was home.

Violet had been in jail part of the time during her absence. Jenny hadn't heard from her once while she was away. "And she's sick," said Jenny looking sad and older. "She's got the *bad* disease. Some man she took up with—" Then Jenny stopped her bitter thoughts, her accusing words, closed her eyes and clenched her hands and said, "Oh God, thank you for helping me to keep on seeing with the eyes of love, thinking with the mind of love and speaking with love."

"What are you going to do?" I asked.

"Hold on to the law of love," said Jenny. "Going to look at Violet with the eyes of love even when she's drunk and abusive. Going to listen to her highest self, her Christ self and keep on knowing she has a power in herself that can change her life for I know what it means to be saved, through Christ."

"You will remember you cannot force Violet?" I cautioned.

"I know I can't change her life," Jenny hastily assured me. "She's got free will. I'll remember that. But I can work with God to bring her to her better senses. God has a stake in the matter. I'm not alone in this. And I am going to keep that circle of love around her. It brought her home like you said it would. My job is to have faith and to keep on working."

"Keep on remembering that with God all good things are possible," I said.

"Oh, I know. The reason I came was to tell you that you can take me off your worry list and put me on your thank-God list."

"Oh, Jenny," I cried, impulsively throwing my arms around her. "Don't you know I already have you on that list! Don't you realize I know beyond a doubt that you will forever go forward without turning back? Didn't you believe me when I told you that before?"

"Yes'um," said Jenny calmly. "I knew you thought I would make out with Nellie all right. But I figured you could be mistaken in what I'd do when Violet came home. Now I know you were right in that too."

Then Jenny said something I never shall forget. Out of the mouth of this uneducated woman came words of purest wisdom, proving that not from books or other people, but from God through love, come our greatest teachings about life. Jenny looked pensive a moment, lost in thought, and then said, "I know what it means when it says in the Bible 'God will wipe away all tears.'"

I urged her to explain it to me.

"It does not mean that we have to wait until we die to get a reward, happiness and relief. It means when we really *find God,* there will be no more tears for we will then know we are safe and sure no matter how black things look. It means we really are safe all the time and when we once find out that fact, our tears are over. That is why I ain't crying about Violet. Knowing about the Spirit of everything being good wiped away my tears before I knew I needed them. It's all settled. Even about Harry, all the world, all my tomorrows, everybody, everything that will ever happen to me. There's no more need ever to cry again except for joy."

So at last I was content to close her file for I knew Jenny was safe forever. Whenever I think of her I always say "Thank you, God, for the privilege of having known her." She taught me much.

And what about you, my friend? Are you trying to speak and listen with love? Have you yet discovered that the only way to draw love into your life is first to *send out* love?

Ask several of your friends how your voice sounds to them. Does it have tone qualities of love, or is it sharp, rasping, strident? If so, change your thinking and your voice will change in kind. Have a record made of your voice. Study it. If it does not carry tones of cheerfulness, joy in living, and at the same time sound calm and soothing, if it is not poised and controlled, look to your total attitude toward life and you will find what is wrong.

And how do you listen? Impatiently? Do you give your speaker the feeling that you are in a hurry and want to be rid of him? Do you frown and appear to be irritated when others talk to you? How do you listen to world news? To good news? To bad news? Check, and you

will be able to tally up pretty accurately your total attitude toward life.

Add to your notes this affirmation:

*I speak and listen with love and love speaks and
listens to me.*

CHAPTER SIX

Think with the Mind of Love

WHEN we learn to think with the mind of love, all else in our life will straighten out. If we could only start our life-changing program by such thinking, we would not consciously have to take the other steps of seeing, hearing and speaking with love. They would be taken automatically.

Few of us, however, can start at the top. Most of us will find we have to take the simple hourly exercises of actually trying to bring our *desires, actions* and *beliefs* under the rule of good and growth for all, in order to build up a consciousness, or *awareness,* of love as the moving spirit of the universe. The daily attempt to speak, listen and look with love may seem to be a very small beginning. But if persisted in, it will lead beyond the mere awareness of the spirit of love to actual thought in harmony with that spirit. This in turn will lead to higher states of consciousness. Eventually it results in willingness to work with God and the ability to do so. When we work with God we cannot fail either in this world or in any world to come.

To think with love means to think with honesty, courage, and fearlessness; to think of all life, including ourselves, as unlimited and good in spirit; to think with kindness, tolerance, and forgiveness, about all that we know to be good. Such thoughts naturally produce acts that are progressive and good. They generate a belief in good. These acts and this faith in turn bring progressive good into our lives and affairs. Until we can think with the mind of love we shall find, as Paul says, all else avails us nothing. As we think, so we are, so we act and so others do unto us.

The whole character of our lives, our attitude about all things, is a direct result of what we think about God. On our real belief about God depends what we think about ourselves, our fellowmen, about health, wealth, happiness, work, the nature of the universe, the question of the existence of good and evil powers and of life after death. In all our thought, we are either thinking with God, nature, and things as they are, or we are thinking against them. When we think against the nature of things as they are, we develop a belief in two powers one of which is evil with its force to overcome good, or God. Once we so divide our house, as Jesus warned, the whole structure of our being is in danger.

We may do no evil but that alone will not save us. Job did no evil. He merely *believed in* it and *so feared* it. What he feared came upon him through the doctrine of the law of creation "after its kind." The story of Job is the story of the human soul in travail to give birth to a consciousness of God as all good. It is the story of every childlike man's struggle to think in accord with the parent, God mind of love by putting aside the human mind of superstition, fear and belief in two powers. It is one of the most dramatic stories in print and should be studied by all who desire to change their lives through knowledge of spiritual laws and how to live within them.

Like Job we can all cry "what I feared came upon me." For fear absorbs some of our most concentrated thinking. It is the strongest kind of belief in evil. We stop fearing only when we learn to think with love. Nothing less than obedience to the love commandments ever can still our fears. Nothing less than understanding them can put us in tune with the universe. When we finally see what Job eventually saw, that the Spirit of all is both *good and unlimited,* then like Job we shall receive more than we had "in the beginning," for we shall know how to draw it to us.

When we fail to think with love we leave ourselves open to two grave dangers. The first and lesser of the two is that we *fail to draw to ourselves all the good we could have.* Here is an example:

A business man came to me for help. He had been a church member all his life, and his parents before him had been church members all their lives. They were good, honest and upright people. The man was very poor in spite of the fact that he owned his own small business which he ran with scrupulous honesty. He could not afford to pay his office help what other shops paid for the same work, and yet, as he often boasted, they stayed on year after year "because they liked him."

In interviewing the employees I discovered most of them were afraid to leave him for higher pay elsewhere because they feared they would never get "another boss quite as congenial and easy to work for as Ed." The law of correspondences was working. Those employees were just as afraid of life as their employer. Ed was torn between being happy at their loyalty and grieved over his inability to pay them more. He was constantly worried and annoyed about high prices generally and especially about the high salaries he was forced to pay his union help.

His business friends called him "Good old Ed." They

trusted him with their secrets, their wives and their money. He merited their trust. But Ed complained to me that they had flourished, owned fine homes and powerful cars. He said, "I know they are no smarter than I am, do not work half so hard and many of them are very questionable in their business and personal dealings. Some of them are downright dishonest. Yet they grow richer, and I grow poorer every year." Ed wanted to know what was wrong with him that the hand of God was so against him.

In church Ed sang about being a worm of the dust, feeble and frail, and he thought of himself as such. His favorite and oft repeated remark was "As my father always said, I'd rather be good and poor than rich and evil."

With all his history before me it was easy to see why Ed and his parents before him, who were equally talented, hard working and honest, had remained poor. For Ed's *thoughts were not with making money.* His mind actually was *against* it. His thoughts, his whole heart, centered on *being good.* And in his secret heart he could not accept money as good no matter how greatly he desired it, how badly he needed it, nor how much he talked about it. Ed secretly believed money was evil. His parents had so believed and so taught him. He thought that anyone had to be a little evil if they were to acquire abundance and that most people were very evil if they had managed to create a fortune. He was living up to his and his father's life motto: he was *good and poor!*

Ed did not think with the mind of love which is all creative, generous beyond our wildest hopes, prolific, abundant, eager to serve and promote the welfare of man. Ed thought against the very nature of love. He thought in terms of scarcity, limitation and poverty.

When I said, "You have no faith in God, yourself nor your fellowmen," he was shocked to speechlessness. While I had him at a disadvantage, I hammered home a few more truths he needed to know if he was to right his life and affairs. "You do not really love God, your fellowmen or yourself. You are actually thumping your chest and thanking God that you are not as sinful as other men. You wear your self-inflicted poverty which robs your employees, your family and yourself as a badge of honor, as a mark of moral superiority. You believe in a God of poverty and punishment. You are making God in your own image and likeness. You think God is dealing unfairly with you, who are honest. You believe He is prospering evil men, and you are very much hurt because He does not punish them and prosper you instead."

After Ed had recovered from the stabs of my pointed facts, he began to realize that harsh as they were, my words were truth. Only after his confession could he begin to right his life and affairs. He learned there is no value whatever in any material thing whether it is gold or a clod of clay. The value lies in what we think about them. Real values are spiritual and never material. That is why Jesus instructed us to seek first the kingdom of God (the place where the spirit of love dwells) in order to find this inner power by which we can create all the good we shall ever need. That is why He taught that we do not have to envy others.

Ed learned that gold and a lump of clay are equally good and that things are acquired through using the powers given us whether or not these things are good or evil. We can get things through an evil desire and purpose and put them to an evil use quite as readily as we can achieve good by good for good. But we must *pay the penalty for evil.* Evil means anything that is contrary to all good and to all growth toward that good.

Ed was using the power of creating to create poverty for himself. His business friends were using the same power to create good for themselves. Ed desired to be good. He asked, thought, and prayed to be good. He believed that he was good, far better than most men. But he also believed that in order to be good he had to be poor. Ed believed money to be evil. He wanted nothing to do with evil. So the *law kept money away from him at his own request!*

Ed's business friends desired things, worked for them, asked for them, believed they would receive them, loved and welcomed them. They loved money. They saw no evil in money. They thought of it as all good, in fact, about the highest good they could obtain. They expected money to come to them, and asked for it by word, deed and thought. Not a one of those successful business men thought of himself as being a worm of the dust, feeble or frail. True, some of them were breaking the laws of love in their desires and acts, thoughts and words. Ed was right in thinking that the illness, worry, tragedies and the drinking of some of his friends grew out of their efforts to "make a pile of money." Their inner Lord (conscience) was angry with them. Ed finally saw that his own inner Lord was angry with him for remaining in poverty, for underpaying his good and faithful employees (one of them had not had a raise in ten years) , for failing to see God's works as good, and for failing to call on, believe in and use the abundance provided him from the "beginning of the world."

Eventually Ed got it into these words: "It is a sin to remain poor when God has supplied us with such abundance for the asking."

Failure to claim and use that which is ours is the lesser danger of failing to think with love. There is a greater danger in that by failing to think with love, we leave ourselves susceptible to plotting against God, or the nature of good.

There is no neutral course. We are for or against good. We may be ignorantly against good as was Ed. When we are knowingly against good, we set up a private power all our own in opposition to God's plans for good for all men and think we can outwit God. Oh, we never get it into those words. We just become spiritual outlaws with a "might makes right" motto of life. We learn to use the doctrine of the law of creation "after its kind" on the level of sheer will power. We use it to overcome all those below our own level of understanding. We see this done every day in the form of "sales psychology." For example, we see some of our best art and brains put to work for the advertising of alcoholic liquor.

Once we are inclined toward evil for personal gain, we begin to ride rough-shod over our fellowmen until they stop us or until we put a rope around our own necks. This latter we always do eventually when we begin to think we have a power greater than the power of good and that we can use it to get what we desire of life no matter what the consequences to others. Whether we know it or not such thinking always shows. And it bears fruit, even unto the third and fourth generation.

Here is an example of how it works out:

A woman came to me about her grandson, aged 8. She had returned from Europe after a long stay during which her sole purpose had been to find happiness. She failed in this, she said, and came back to learn that her only grandchild had been committed to an institution for the mentally sick.

"He's no more crazy than you are," she declared hotly.

Much questioning revealed the fact that her anger was really against her former son-in-law (the boy's father) and that man's second wife. "They had him put in because they wanted to get rid of him," she stormed in fine fury.

The facts were these: the boy's father and mother had been divorced when he was about five after many court and private battles, involving bitter and unsavory accusations. The boy had been awarded to his mother. She remarried. The step-father did not like the child, was jealous of the attention his mother gave him and refused to have the boy around. The mother then sent him to live with his father and his father's people. These people hated the boy's mother, constantly maligned her and tried to "turn him against her."

Next, the boy's father remarried and the step-mother did not want the boy for his behavior had grown so "bad she couldn't manage him." The father then wanted the mother to take the boy back. But she, angered at all the stories told against her and at the child's attitude to her because of them, refused to take him. So he ended up in a boarding school.

Soon the boy had set out on a program of cruelty that shocked the adults around him. He tortured his pets until they had to be taken from him. He played horrible tricks on nurses, servants and teachers. He finally was committed to the institution as "the only thing that can be done with him." His latest escapade there had been to evade his guards, find a little frog on the grounds and cut it up into bits while it was still alive because he "liked to see it be hurt."

The child's difficulties had begun when he was about three and a half, with stuttering and violent fits of rage.

"I just don't know what got into T——" said his grandmother. "He's bright. And he was a sweet baby the last time I saw him." She had not seen him since he was three years old.

"Hate, hurt and a desire for revenge have got into him," I said. "Not knowing a higher law of life, the poor child is trying to strike back and take an eye for an eye and a tooth for a tooth. He is trying to protect himself in the only way he knows. He behaves like a savage because he believes the world is a savage place. If he cannot hurt people larger than himself then he must 'save face' and get revenge by hurting something smaller. This makes him feel secure in an insecure world. It proves his powers to himself. Since he does not have the security of love, he must try to get it by making others afraid of him. He is only upholding the law of self-preservation on his level of understanding."

The history back of the child covered two generations of two families which had lived their lives and created their fortunes outside the law of loving God, their fellowmen and their highest selves.

Both pairs of the child's grandparents had been divorced. The grandfathers had piled up dollar fortunes by any means at hand, proud of their wit and cunning in cheating partners, underpaying their employees and being unfaithful to God, their fellowmen and their own wives. They betrayed trusts placed in them and yet seemed to flourish like the green bay tree, "always being two jumps ahead of their opponent" said the grandmother. Each side of the house hated and mistrusted the other, indulging in quarrels, accusations and general strife. They tormented their own flesh, as the Bible puts it. Their enemies were the thoughts and beliefs which led to their acts.

Thus the child's parents had been brought up to think against the laws of good for all. They belonged to a "fashionable social set," which spent its time traveling, drinking, dressing up, dancing and hunting for thrills. The dollar fortunes acquired were so substantial that neither of the young parents ever had to think about earning money. They had never heard about the desirability of laying up treasures in heaven, much less did they know how to go about doing so. They spent their lives trying to find a happiness, a meaning to life which forever eluded them. They knew so little of the laws of good that they made one tragic mistake after another which would have to be rectified some day if they were to have happiness, peace of mind or soundness of body.

The grandmother had come to me for help, hoping to have the child released to her, and saying, "He'd never hurt me. I'd find a good strong nurse who would scare him, control him and break him of those habits."

"He's already been broken too badly now," I reminded her. "What he needs is building up. He needs to be persuaded, loved and shown, not controlled."

The grandmother's real desire was not to help the child. What she wanted was to "get even" with her hated former son-in-law and that second wife of his who had "brazenly stolen him away from her daughter and caused the divorce in the first place."

I explained that in my opinion there was only one thing to do that would help the child and that was truly

to love him and let him know that he was loved. The
first step in helping him is to get him to *feel safe and
wanted.*"

"But don't you think that my former son-in-law
should be punished—?"

After my four hours' talk to her, she went away almost
as ignorant of the law of love as she had been when she
had come. I was wearied in spirit, sure the whole time
had been wasted. But once again I learned that no honest effort ever is wasted. Not all the seed had fallen on
barren ground. Enough had lodged in fertile soil to
make her return not long after, looking ten years older,
to say, "I shall never have another moment's rest as long
as T—— is in that institution. I have been talking to
his grandfather, my first husband, the father of my
daughter, and he feels the same way. And I guess his
grandparents on his father's side are pretty unhappy
too. We can't get him released."

Nor could the child's parents ever drink so much or
pursue pleasure so madly that they did not wonder
what the child was doing at that moment, whether he
was trying to cut a little frog into bits or planning the
destruction of a fellow human being. The end product
of four grandparents, two parents and two enormous
fortunes had not grown to be a flower of civilization and
a credit to his heritage, but a child monster, something
so dreadful it was talked about only in whispers.

"Why did it have to happen to us?" the grandmother
whimpered bitterly. "My only grandchild! The sole heir
to all our money!"

It didn't happen. It resulted. The corrupt tree does
not produce good fruit. Good trees produce good fruit.
If we want figs and not thistles we must first produce a

fig tree. God is never mocked, and love is the nature of God, the highest law of the universe. We tinker with that law, try to outwit it, at the cost of our lives.

"Oh, but that is an extreme case," someone may say.

Yes, it is. But between that extreme case and the tiniest shady dealing against a brother, the smallest thought outside the law of love, veering from the path of right and good for all, we can see human wrecks of unhappiness, failure, grief, disappointment, sickness, poverty and every manner of unwanted results all attributable to one thing: failure to understand the nature of love, failure to *think with* love. As we think, so we are, we do and we have.

We cannot too often remember that the purpose of all human life is growth toward greater good. This is accomplished by using our free will to *desire* and to *work* for good. This is the process Paul refers to as being transformed by the renewing of our mind. For it is a mental process. We grow from the inside. By thinking with love we refine our minds, bodies and souls. We put off the flesh man. We put on the Christ man, the free will, the liberated soul bound only by our soul's desire, and unfettered by instincts and flesh rule. Hence Paul says "Christ in you the hope of glory." It is by trying to use this highest Christ mind within us, the mind of pure love, that we turn matter into spirit, corruption into honesty and death into eternal life.

If we want to learn how to think with love, let us study the life and works of Jesus Christ. For He was the perfected man, the very Spirit of Love become flesh, the kind of man all men may some day be when they have learned how to live within the laws of love and choose to do so to the extent that Jesus knew and chose. That is what evolution is striving for—the man perfected in Christ.

With all our hearts, minds and souls we can rely on the teachings of Jesus! This man of Nazareth was indeed the forerunner of the future, evolved man. He was the first Christ man on earth whose coming was foreseen and foretold by prophets for generations. Jesus is an example of what a man is when he is truly "born of God," or the Spirit of Love. "Love is of God; and every one that loveth is begotten of God." (*John* 4:7) Christ is the pattern of what the future man can be after he has learned what love is and is willing to be born again with no ambition, desire, plan or thought *outside of love.*

How long it will take the whole human race to catch hold of the truths Jesus taught, to reach the height of love Jesus reached, no one can say. Du Noüy, in his great work *Human Destiny* says Jesus may have been a million years ahead of the race. If we had a million years on earth in which to observe what happens when we start to think and to live contrary to all good, we'd see that we cannot cheat the law by act, the letter, nor by intent, the spirit. We can simply accept it now as truth beyond question and start to live within the highest of all laws watching miracles of good happen to us and for us.

We need not understand the perfect love of the Father as Jesus understood it in order to be able to call on and use it. We have only to take Jesus' advice and become as trusting little children, realizing that there is a power, a Divine plan so stupendous, so far beyond our present ability to understand that we cannot possibly cope with it. But we can trust. We can desire to be good. We can control our thoughts, desires and acts. If we do that, we shall be growing toward God and that is all we need to do or to know at this stage of our evolution.

We have now considered the four steps necessary in order to establish love as the highest law of our lives. To establish, says Webster, means to "prove and cause to be accepted as true; to put beyond doubt or dispute." To use the methods as given in the last four chapters is to establish the law. It now remains for us to take the final steps, *working with and trusting* the law. In a sense we are working with and trusting the law in all our affirmations and daily exercises.

Let's pause here and talk about you and your problem. What do you think about most of the time? Write it down. Now examine it carefully. Do you think about the *lack* or the *fulfillment* of that lack? Do you think about good news or bad news as it comes up daily? Are you angry with anyone? If so, "Let not the sun go down upon your wrath." The angry thoughts and feelings you hold against another are hurting you and keeping you from making your demonstration.

Is there anyone who has a just and rightful claim upon your heart, time, and money which you have not met? If so, go to meet it and do not hope to make your demonstration in full until you have done so.

We have man-made laws which demand punishment for the adult who contributes to the delinquency of a minor. Likewise, there are spiritual laws which will punish the more highly developed person who uses his mentality to overcome a lesser mind for evil purposes. If your work requires of you any such domination, leave it. Attach yourself to work that is spiritually good, in line with God's plan of good for all men, or you will eventually suffer.

It is impossible to feel absolutely free and on an equal footing with all men until we are "right with God" within our own mind and know that we are. When we learn to think with the mind of love, we shall have no more problems, no more fears. Therefore, my friend, you do not face as many problems as there are hours in the day or days in your life. There is only one problem: learn how to work with God.

Go to your closet or meditation room. Think over the facts of existence as you now know them. Come again to the decision to let the very Spirit or intent of good rule your life. Then say, *"Father, I earnestly ask that the same mind be in me which was in Christ Jesus. I desire to learn how to think with love."*

Then live up to your prayer. Try to see good all around you. Try to relax and be happy knowing you are in God's care, knowing that no matter how many mistakes you have made, or yet may make, they can all be forgiven by your calling on God for forgiveness. The very desire to lead a better life is prayer in itself, and does not go unanswered. If the road sometimes seems long and you seem to be making little or no progress, do not despair. Struggle is normal for man, until he has finally learned to think with love. Each struggle carries you just that much farther ahead. The effort to be good accumulates good.

So look up, and be lifted up. Keep on thinking good thoughts, desiring good and good will come as day follows night. And always, always be of good cheer!

.

PART THREE

How to Work with
the Law of Love

CHAPTER SEVEN

To Produce Wealth

WE HAVE seen how to establish the law of love as the highest law of our lives, and now we must go farther and actually start to work with this great creative force which we call love. For just knowing about this power which can create a universe or a man, restore health or quicken the dead is not enough to change our lives. We must actually *put it to use.*

Since most people think money is the answer to every problem (which it most certainly is not) let's talk about how to work with desire for all good to produce wealth. Here is an example of how it can be done.

In the depression days a few years back a young man came to me for help. Not long out of college he had come west looking for some ideal he felt he had not found. He was unhappy and lately had been ill, though there seemed nothing organically wrong with him. He had attacks of dizziness and stomach sickness. He was, he said, "very sick of poverty."

In working with problems of others I take as truth or spiritual law, Jesus' promise that where two are agreed concerning a thing it will be done unto them as they ask. We then ask, in prayer. Our first step is to agree. But this young man confessed he knew very little about prayer. He never had had a prayer answered and did not think he could pray for abundance and receive it.

He did not discount prayer as he was sure others "got something out of it," but it was "too deep for him."

This student was a good man. He had been brought up in church but said he had never gotten much out of it. He attended occasionally now that he was away from home because he felt that this much respect was due his parents who were ardent church workers. He felt rather guilty about his non-attendance. His parents were poor and had struggled all their lives. The young man had worked his way through school and felt he could not accept his parent's views on the blessings of poverty as a means of enriching the spirit. The Old Testament was a hodge-podge to him, much of it "disgusting, a recital of murder, rape, war, greed, ambition and too much talk about one's enemies and revenge but with some good advice here and there."

He liked the New Testament. He had read some of my published work concerning the spiritual laws and had come to me because he was "convinced there was a better way to handle the affairs of life" than the way in which he then was handling them.

We began our work on the agreement that if others could and did learn the mysteries of prayer as an aid in solving the every day problems of life then he, the student, could do likewise. We took as our promise the following:

"Therefore I say unto you, what things soever ye desire, when ye pray, believe that ye receive them and ye shall have them." (Jesus in *Mark* 11:24)

Asked to state his desire in one sentence the young man said, "I desire to get rid of poverty. It is the only real problem I have."

"Your real problem," I corrected, "is to learn *how to create wealth*. Poverty is nothing. Your desire is to create a fortune. We need not bother to think about how to get rid of nothing."

He agreed. I then explained the rules involved:

"First, your purpose for wanting wealth must be spiritually legal, within the law of love. Second, you must desire to create a fortune. Next, you must act. To act includes asking with your prayers. It also includes your every thought, word and deed. All these must come within the law of love. Then you must believe. You must have faith in the success of your project. You must have such unbounded faith in it that you will become as happy as though *it had been done*. This will require a perpetual attitude of happy expectancy which will come only if and when you can truly believe in God's love not only for you, but for all men.

"Finally, you must be *grateful*. If you are grateful, your very pores will open to receive good. Every brain cell will be stimulated to both giving and receiving good. For it is a spiritual law that a grateful man shall abound in blessings. Gratitude includes *sharing your time, your love and your money*. You must do this cheerfully. Your inner Lord loves cheerful giving and also, cheerful living. There is a spiritual law involved. To give cheerfully stimulates your consciousness to earn more. It takes away fear. It makes you confident that there is more to be had where that which you are giving away came from. Being cheerful is trusting God. You must also bless your money, love and bless (desire good for) all whom you contact in your work. Above all else, you must actually desire a fortune, care about it with all the fervor of which your heart is capable, in order to create it."

"That," said the student, "is a very large order!"

"A very large bill of goods is what you hope to receive," I reminded him. "And you will get what you *desire,* order, *pray for* and *believe* in."

We then took stock of what he had in hand. This too is a spiritual law—start with what you have and make the first move. He was working for a housing firm. He was surprised to learn that his unhappiness and his inclination to stomach sickness grew out of his secret disapproval of his firm's policies which were bad to say the least.

"Guess I am just too critical, sort of holier than thou," the student said, when we traced his last attack of stomach sickness to the time he had just learned of the sad plight of an elderly widow his firm had swindled.

"It is all very legal," the student explained. "The old lady lost her suit in court, lost her money, lost hope. She never will get the home she thought she'd get. She is broke. This is the way the firm does business. The whole policy of the company is to trade on the ignorance of victims who sign tricky contracts which they don't understand." He explained the working of it in detail. A subsequent check-up showed his statements to be true. The firm was barely right legally and shamefully wrong morally and spiritually.

"Be glad it makes you sick at your stomach," I said. "The stomach is sympathetic. It is an accepter of food. Digested food becomes a part of the living body. So with ideas. You are deliberately choosing right and openly refusing to accept wrong. Even your stomach revolts. To be revolted at the injustices to your fellowmen and desirous of doing something about them is to be working with love. It shows us you have a conception of that three-phase or perfect love which includes all men, nature, or God, and yourself. So be glad."

He wanted "to do the right thing," and was inclined

to think it meant staying with that firm and trying to "bring the men up to a higher level."

But it would take more courage, understanding, faith and work than the student could manage to bring the firm up to his own high standard. He had no moral right to try as long as they did not want to comply with the law of love. For they had free will. If they desired to attempt evil and hoped to cheat the spiritual laws of love, they had the privilege of trying. But sooner or later all that they were doing that was "not built by the Father" would have to be torn down.

So the student decided to shake the dust of that unbelieving firm from his feet and set out for another job. His history showed me that his outstanding talent was a great and natural love for people. He loved to meet people, loved to talk to them, to serve them. He could go a very long way in forgiving and was not critical by nature. He had good taste, good judgment and much discrimination in selecting goods and wares having to do with housing. He said he "just loved anything having to do with a new home." I advised him to take a sales job and to quit the office work which he had been educated to do and so disliked.

The student was afraid to change from a type of work he knew to one he did not know. But he admitted he felt his present employment "held him back; offered little chance for growth."

"Take a job that you can *love*, one that will let you *grow*," I advised. "Your soul will convict you, accuse and nag you until you do take steps to grow. If you deny it too often, too firmly and too long the pangs may seem to become less. But that will be because you are turning your back on them. They never really die. You may take to drink, to gambling, to some other vice, or you may compromise, do most anything to 'save face' but if you do, eventually it will show up in your mind as deep unhappiness and in your body as ill health. You will remain poor all the days of your life. Put your talent to work or suffer! You naturally *love* things to do with a new home. Get a sales job in some field having to do with your natural desires, *work with love*."

To this he agreed. He already had developed an attitude of happy expectancy which further aligned him with nature, helped him to join his individual force with the creative force of the universe. We are never so near God as when we are truly happy.

Finally a new job opened, but the student was discouraged. It offered only eighteen dollars a week. He had been receiving twenty-five. His hours would be longer. He would be working six days a week instead of five. "Isn't that going backward?" he worried.

But it was sales work in line with his talents. He liked the firm's policies and its personnel. "I could work there with pride," he reported.

"Could you feel you were working *with God?* Would you *love* and *desire to promote* the work? Would you *grow?*" I asked.

He answered yes to all three and accepted the position.

We then began to work with the law of increase, the one which Jesus worked with when he multiplied the loaves and fishes. We accepted as a fact "all that the Father hath" is ours and that it is our Father's good pleasure to give us that for which we ask. "The nature of life is abundance. We have but to ask to receive it."

To help him in his prayer program I made up the following jingle for him which he was to use hundreds of times a day:

"Three dollars a day
Is my present rate of pay
But the more I learn
The more I earn,
For I'm learning God's loving and limitless way!"

Poor poetry but sound sense. It is a statement of a spiritual truth. It is recognizing the laws of growth. It is working with the spiritual law of cause and effect, with the law of creation's doctrine "after its kind." This alone would not have been enough. The big thing, the underlying principle, was that he had to be operating within the law of love. Also, he had to know beyond any doubt that there was nothing to oppose him! I warned him that the instant he doubted he then began to neutralize his efforts and would demonstrate according to his *fear* instead of according to his *desire*. He was praying for the way, the wisdom and the work by which he would create a fortune, and he had to believe that they had already been received.

During the early time of his new job the student began to study his Bible seriously. Each time he read, he admitted that he "saw a new truth which before had escaped him." One day he reported that he now knew Jesus meant wisdom, courage and actual guidance, when He said "all that the Father hath is thine." A little later, he began to realize that he already had all he needed within himself, and that he must merely bring it forth, a process of recognition quite as much as creation.

Presently the student was put on a commission basis, and in a short time he was earning first fifty, then seventy-five and finally a hundred dollars a week. At each new increase of pay he changed the amount in the first line of his jingle. One day he said, "Look, if I can earn a hundred dollars a week what's to keep me from earning a hundred dollars a day as long as I keep within the laws of love? Why should there be any limit? As long as I work with God, I am doing His work, carrying out His Will. Why wouldn't God be pleased with me and rejoice in my growth and help me further?"

This showed us he had some learning yet to do before he could get away from the old idea of a personal God, the idea of a Superman, a deity made in man's own image and likeness. But he eventually did come to accept God as the Spirit, the Cause of all there is, rather than as a person. Then he saw that he must think not of having God work with him, but of raising his own consciousness to that place where he *could see that he was working with God*, the creative Spirit of all good and of principles already established.

The world always pays top wages to top performers of a work that blesses all. Working for love always brings more money than merely working for pay.

"If the laws of growth, abundance and increase work on a small scale for one individual, why will they not work on a very large scale, for all the world?" the student earnestly inquired. "Why couldn't we change our economic system by this same law?"

"We could," I assured him. "The power that was able to create a universe could certainly create all the things needed by the life which it also created, loves and placed within that universe. Man has been provided for from the beginning of the world. Certainly we could learn how to work with the creative spirit of all good and create a heaven on earth."

"Then why don't we?" he wondered.

"For lack of enough love, enough right purpose, enough desire to help others," I replied. "People as a whole do not understand the nature of the Spirit of the Universe. They believe in poverty, bad luck, and set them above the power of good. They try to take from others because they believe in scarcity yet all the time the natural law is one of abundance. We see it in sands, seed and everywhere that life abounds. Abundance is a part of the evidence of the law of love. Love always is lavish, gives, provides richly. Belief in that law opens the door to abundance. You are as unlimited as you believe yourself to be."

"Then I am unlimited, period," he said seriously.

Before we go on with his story, let us stop here and consider the points which had to do with his success and will have to do with the success of any individual who accepts as truth the promise "All that the Father hath is thine" and then sets out to call upon it.

This young man's purpose was right and good. He had faith before he tried his works. He did not just sit down and dream but worked to create a fortune. Finally, he greatly desired, and *loved* abundance.

In working, he looked with the eyes of love, listened and spoke with love. He thought with the mind of love. He was frank, kind, honest to all and happily expectant. That was trusting love. He loved the people who came to buy from him. He cared about their problems, hopes, desires, even about their families and let them know he cared. He cared to please them and they loved and trusted him. They couldn't keep from it! For it is the way of love. They came back for more purchases and brought their sisters, their cousins and their aunts. And oh, how he loved his work! How he *loved to earn!*

He worked with gratitude. He blessed every cent that

came to his hands, called it God, or good in substance, and saw it as evidence of the power of good loving him and blessing him. So he in turn blessed his money on receiving it and on sending it out. He accepted blessing as a part of the established principles of increase. He loved to spend. As he worked, his vision enlarged. He kept on thinking about things that needed to be done—for people. The more he thought with the mind of love the farther his own mind reached out into time and space. One day he said, "Look, if this law of desire for increase works in this way, why couldn't we use love to increase *all good?* I mean like working with animals and plants and the very molecules of substance. By loving, praising, blessing we could increase crops and improve the soil. No country on earth need be poverty stricken!"

"I am sure the time will come when man will not need crops and the round of seed time and harvest," I assured him. "When there is enough love in the world, enough desire to promote the progressive good of all men, and when individuals reach a high enough place in love and purity of self and purpose, then they will learn to produce directly from the ether substance all around us as Jesus did. That is exactly what He promised men should do some day. But it will come only through love. The secrets of the universe cannot be revealed to fools nor to evil men. For such men cannot hear the Voice of Love speaking. They do not know how to listen to God."

In all this the student, you see, was seeking enlightenment for his total life, eternity, and not just for the problem at hand—that of creating a fortune. He had begun to grasp the fact that life is a wholeness. Of course, all he learned he immediately put to work on his present problem.

From the first the student had tithed the accustomed ten per cent of his income. As his earnings increased he considered it "not enough" and gave away several times the ten per cent for good causes. In giving he always used the Unity School of Christianity form of blessing: "Divine Love, through me, blesses and multiplies this offering," which is exactly what happens. That affirmation actually sets a force into motion which will fulfill the dictates of the speaker's words "after its kind" unless through fear, neglect or a decision contrary to love, the speaker sets up another order to cancel the first request.

As he believed, he received. By his words he was justified. The windows of heaven were opened up to him. His fortunes doubled, trebled. His last account to me was that he had earned fifty-two thousand dollars the year before, and he added, "I am still growing. I have no moral right to do less, for every day I see more and more clearly what love means and how to work with it."

The student also received understanding and all manner of good that surpasses silver or gold. He had love, peace, harmony, friends, happiness and contentment. The nearest he ever came to grief or worry was his knowledge that his way of life could be used by all men and that so few were using it. Like Jesus, he too sighed deeply in his spirit that men so hurt and impoverished themselves by their lack of faith in good, by their ignorance of the laws and by their attempts to break them.

We shall not get the full benefit from the foregoing case unless we compare it with the facts of the case of his first employers. The corrupt firm was also proving the truth of the law of creation. The men for whom the student had worked were also justified and condemned by their own words. These men thought in terms of scarcity and limitations. These became a law unto them. For what we believe is always a law to us though it may not be a law to anyone else in the whole world.

The men in this firm saw all business as a "cut throat" affair. They believed that any man would "outdeal" them if he could. They admired a man who could get the better of another because to them, that was "being smart," and "good business." But they entertained murderous rages against those who got the better of themselves which should have warned them that something was wrong with their conception of the laws. They always thought of themselves as cheated and outwitted, if they were not quicker, sharper and shrewder than their opponent. And to them, every man was their opponent. They had no conception of the brotherhood of man, none of God as a power of good. They believed a power of evil in the minds of others was able to overcome them.

Those men did not know the secret of the law of increase. They did not realize that love never robs one source in order to supply another but either exchanges or creates something new. Their method was to cheat, lie, steal and misrepresent in order to acquire. Their specialty was in preying on those of less intelligence and education than they possessed.

By their words they were justified and by their words they were condemned. The two owners of the firm were neatly swindled out of all they had by two others who were engaged in the same business and who believed the way to acquire wealth is to be clever enough or powerful enough to take it away from your fellowmen.

I cannot leave this subject without a reminder that

there are two methods of producing wealth. One is to create and store it. But this leaves it open to rust, moths and thieves who break in and steal. Until we actually overcome all fear of poverty, our created and stored wealth is always in danger of being dissipated. So long as we have a fear, we shall make mistakes and be in danger of drawing to us in accordance with that fear. God Himself cannot keep us prosperous when we think of losing what we have. Generally speaking, a desire to store up wealth is proof in itself of a fear of the future, a doubt about our power to earn, a doubt about God's ability and intention to provide.

The ideal is to learn to create a constant supply or rather to recognize the fact that it already exists and is at hand. This does not mean that we should sit and indulge in wishful thinking. It means that we should desire, ask, act and believe without worry, fear or hesitation. Anyone who can find a way to serve their fellowmen can make all the money they need.

Some day our scientists will discover the way to create in rapid chain fashion as they now destroy with the atomic bomb. There is more than enough for human needs, more than we can see or imagine. The human race learned how to kill men long before it learned how to save their lives. We should not give up hope that we shall yet become more constructive as time goes by for we shall learn more and more of love. Eventually, we shall learn to use the law of creation as easily, as safely and for as good results as we now use fire.

Meantime, you, the individual, need not wait to create all the prosperity you need. You have the formula as given in the spiritual laws. Go to work—for love and with love!

Remember: Love is the force that creates good. Its

nature is to progress. It always creates more good than there was "in the beginning."

Add to your notes:

"Father, I thank thee for my instant, constant and abundant supply."

CHAPTER EIGHT

To Restore and Maintain Health

THE farther we go in our studies of the spiritual laws the more we shall find the tremendous part our feelings play in our lives. This is because our feelings set forces into motion by filling our thoughts and acts with power. Feelings go deeper than reason.

Feelings of love and of hate are some of the strongest known to man. Each of these produce after their kind. *Love is the greatest healing agent yet discovered. More people are sick from lack of love in their lives than from all other causes put together.*

God, the spirit of love, is the power which created and maintains the life of earth. Certainly then He is the power which can heal. A careful study of the Bible and revelations to my own consciousness convince me that there is no hope of eternal life for the individual outside love and that this love must be expressed by the individual. Since love is the extreme desire for the welfare of mankind, we see that God is love, and He can do no more for man than love him, and be no more to man, than the fountain of love! Therefore God Himself cannot save us if we reject love and His plan for all men. God's part has been done to the point where we must intelligently and willingly co-operate. Until we do that, God can go no farther in plans for us. For we have free will. This Jesus preached, and we must believe it if we are to restore our health through love. In fact, we must eventually believe it if we are to continue in evolution and eternal life.

Through psychiatry, psychology, psychoanalysis and psychosomatic medicine the world is rapidly becoming convinced of the truth of Jesus' teachings concerning the spiritual laws as they affect our mental, spiritual and physical health. Summed up we must love or suffer not only unto death, I am convinced, but to "outer darkness."

To restore health we must love God, the essence of all good. If we had enough love, we could be instantly healed. We could close our hospitals for the sick would take up their beds and walk. There would be no accidents for we would love ourselves, our neighbor and the progressive good of all men so much that we would prevent them. For one quick example, we have discovered that most automobile accidents caused by reckless driving are due to the emotions of the driver who hates himself and the world and is unconsciously trying to reek vengeance on himself and others. Industry has learned to look into the emotional life of the employee who meets with accidents. The failing employee often is one who is having troubles with love.

Germs, always present on earth, could not harm us if we vibrated at the high frequency of desire to live and serve which Jesus knew. For example, Dr. Harold G. Wolff, associate professor of Medicine, Cornell University Medical College, announced recently that anger opens the way to the "common cold." He explained how in anger, the germs already present in the nasal tract are enabled to get hold and start infection. The same is true of "fear of danger," he said. If we loved God, ourselves, and our fellowmen enough, we'd overcome all worries and really live. We would lift our minds above the level of microbes and germs.

If we knew as much about the spiritual laws as Jesus knew, we could heal every disease known to man and do so without having first to learn the nature of the disease itself. If we knew those laws we'd know that love, the white hot desire for all good, is the highest law, which other laws challenge in vain.

The Intelligence that created microbes and germs created also the human machine, loves it and knows what it needs to maintain it in perfect running order. That Intelligence is available to all who ask its guidance. But it does not interfere with man's own free will about such matters as germs or bodily health.

There is a Love that has the welfare of human beings at heart. Within man there dwells the very spirit of God, or that same love which is so all mighty, so all seeing and so all caring, that it is aware of even the fall of a sparrow.

Again, there is a purpose in man's being on earth which is far more important to God the Creator than to man the created. The love and intelligence which first desired, and then created the beginnings of man, placing him on earth for a purpose, have led him thus far on his way. They are available to guide all who believe in and ask for such guidance. But God so loved man that he gave him free will, and with that free will man has the choice of *working with love,* God's plan for man, or of refusing to do so. We get right back to where we started from, the two commandments of love. There is no hope for man outside of them.

Love—or suffer!

Recently Dr. Edward Weiss of Temple University Medical School announced that chronic victims of muscular aches and pains without organic ailments were probably suffering from a smoldering grudge against someone close to them. This is a fact to which every faith healer can testify. We have articulated it in the phrase: "Who is the matter with you?"

A woman who suffered sudden attacks of neuritis came to me for help. She had such pains up her arms and in the side of her neck that she could not drive her car, could hardly move her head. She then had to spend long hours resting under the infra-red lamps. These attacks were becoming more frequent, lasting longer and increasing in severity. We traced them to those times when her daughter-in-law came to dinner. She was sure "that woman" was ruining her son's life and had "tricked him into marriage," though the son seemed to be happy indeed. The woman suffered so terribly she was willing, she said, to do anything to be healed forever. But when I told her she'd have to stop her hard, harsh thoughts and feelings about her daughter-in-law, she was sure she could not do it.

I then advised her to stay away from her son's wife to avoid living a lie and pretending a love she did not feel. So she moved to another town. The neuritis attacks fell off to almost nothing. Convinced she was on the road to healing she came back for help. That time I did not spare her but pointed out facts which her own history revealed. I told her that she was really furious with herself because she felt she had failed as a mother and her daughter-in-law had brought her son more happiness as a wife than she had been able to bring to him.

Self-hatred often masks itself as love. The woman was brave and determined. She eventually righted her life and restored her health through love. But it began with herself. Jesus commanded us to love ourselves because self-hatred is a destroyer of health and life. It is impossible to love our brother while we are hating ourselves. It is equally impossible to love ourselves while hating our brother. For to hate our brother is to set a force into motion against ourselves. Hate creates "after its kind."

Another woman came to me for help complaining that her "prayer for perfect and radiant health" had not been answered. She had been "run down" for years, she said, and was always tired, nervous, felt heavy, couldn't sleep, and worried about everything. She was only fifty-two years old but appeared to be about sixty-five. She was intelligent, a college graduate, wife of a professional man. He had heard me lecture and had taken her a copy of my book *Change Your Life Through Prayer* several months before but she had not "had time to read it." Yet she confessed that she spent several hours a day reading murder mysteries and other escape novels.

"What are you running from?" I finally asked when all the evidence before me indicated that she was trying to hide and that her Lord was angry. After some very unvarnished questioning on my part she began to tell me the true facts about her life. Then the trouble stood revealed.

When the woman was about twenty-five years of age her older brother who had served as administrator of their father's estate had cheated her out of part of her inheritance, a sum of less than three thousand dollars. For twenty-seven years thereafter she had silently, but none the less bitterly, hated that brother. This hatred had ruined her complexion, her features, her figure, and her outlook on life, all people, and most of all, herself. For secretly, in her heart, she knew she was wrong.

The truth is that though we may deceive the whole world, we cannot for an instant deceive our own soul. There is a judge within us who can neither be bribed nor swayed, silenced nor fooled. It is our own Christ Mind, the very Spirit of God within ourselves. This I explained to the woman and told her she had to forgive her brother or continue to suffer.

"I don't see why I should," she argued petulantly. "He wronged me. Let him ask my forgiveness. I shall not ask his!"

"Then you cannot expect God to forgive you. It is the law, the way things are made. Forgive your brother or God cannot heal you."

"Forgive *me?* Why, what have *I* done? I haven't done any wrong," she expostulated angrily.

"You have committed a greater crime against yourself and your brother than he has committed against you," I said and opened my Bible and read to her:

"Whosoever hateth his brother is a murderer" (1 *John* 3:15) and "If any man say, I love God, and hateth his brother he is a liar." (1 *John* 4:20) "And why beholdest thou the mote that is in thy brother's eye but considerest not the beam that is in thine own eye?" (*Matthew* 7:3) "Love your enemies, bless them that curse you, do good to them that hate you, and pray for them which despitefully use you and persecute you." (*Matthew* 5:44) By that time she had put her hands to her face and asked me to stop.

I asked her to read the whole book of *Matthew* when she got home and to read it several times before she came back for a conference. She returned to say she had "discovered facts never before apparent to her," though she had been a church member all her life and still possessed her first Bible. "Somehow I thought of my brother as the sinner, myself as sinned against, and I was put out with God for letting me be cheated."

When she had righted her life, she said "I feel as if I had truly been born again," and just so, she had.

I feel sure that had Christ Jesus been dealing with that woman He would have had only to look at her, and by His great love, His desire to promote her welfare, His deep compassion and forgiveness, He would have communicated to her that He understood. His glance would have conveyed to her that such a petty hatred was unworthy of a human being, persuading her silently to forget, forgive and so, be healed. I feel sure He would have had only to say "Wilt thou?" and she, answering with her inner mind, shamed before His love, inspired by it, would have said, "I will," and would have been instantly made whole. Perhaps Jesus would then have added, "Go your way, sin no more, hate no more, lest a worse thing come upon you, now that you understand the law."

When we reach the place that Jesus reached in His desire to promote the welfare of all men, we too can heal by our words and looks, but long before we have grown that perfect in love, we can heal ourselves and point out the way of restoring health to others. *Love heals.* We have but to set it into motion in our hearts, minds and souls to prove it!

If you have a health problem and wish to be restored to wholeness, start out by thinking, knowing, *that you can be healed!* But unless you actually love health and desire to be healed, no power on earth or in heaven can make you entirely well. God Himself does not usurp your free will. It is your right to be ill if you desire illness.

In working with people who were trying to restore

their health I often have been amazed at how may of them did not recognize the fact that they had no desire to be healed. For example, a man who said he would "give anything" to be cured finally faced the truth that he did not want to be at all for fear he would again fail in his profession. Once well, he would have to go back to work, and he so feared the pain of repeated failure that he actually preferred illness to facing the test again.

Another man who had long received the tender care of his loving family and had enjoyed his suffering because it was "refining his soul," kept on praying for health, being sure to add always, "Lord, if this be good for my soul, and if it is Thy Will, then let me continue to suffer." And the Lord let him. The only positive words in his prayer were "let me contine to suffer." God had given him the free will to choose, and he received according to the choice he made.

Many good, honest and conscientious people suffer needlessly because they actually believe that by so doing they are serving God. They even feel that they have no right to pray for relief saying, "It is the Will of God for me to suffer. It is my duty to suffer patiently and without complaint." These good people do not understand God's Will, or the law of love. If they did, they would know God's Will is the welfare of mankind. Sickness is a sin and the result of a sin which is contrary to love and to God's Will for the welfare of man. It is merely the consequence of a man-made mistake. We have long since outgrown the hair cloth shirt, the sack cloth and ashes, the burnt offering sacrifice as a way of worshiping God. We should discard all their mental equivalents too. Much of our sickness is a hangover from the old idea of humiliating the flesh in order to improve the Soul.

Yet another reason why some are not healed in spite

of their prayers for health lies in their purpose in life. For example, witness the case of an alcoholic with whom I worked—and failed. The man finally admitted that once restored he would go right back to the same old life he had lived before which had brought on his illness in the first place. (Alcoholics are desperately ill persons. The illness is basically a spiritual one which first strikes the mind and then the body of its victim.) That man's inner Christ consciousness was silently reminding him that he would have to change his whole life and for some secret reason of his own which he never could bring himself to confess, he was not willing to do so. Such people simply do not love life. Life to them is not the thrilling experience it should be, but a bewildering affair, burdensome and filled with care and fears. They see no way of changing it, once well, and so they are unconsciously desiring to die. The choice is always ours.

Indifference to life and to others leads to dry rot in ourselves. Hate destroys and eats like an acid. Love alone creates, builds that which is good, fulfills the whole law of life on the physical, mental and spiritual planes alike.

If you have a health problem, the first thing to do is to rid your mind *of all* thoughts contrary to love for all people, including yourself, and God. Then rid your mind of all thoughts contrary to the desire for the good of all. Finally rid your life of all words, deeds, and beliefs contrary to the good of all.

As soon as you wake up in the morning say, *"I believe in the power of the living God within me to heal me and make me whole."* Then consider your words. If you think of that Power within you as being connected with God Mind, all there is, that God Mind can and will instruct you what to do and how to do it in order to be healed. Think of this power that is *alive* within you and intelligent, as creating new cells, carrying off poisons, adjusting parts to the whole, as anything and everything necessary to make you well. Above all, remember this power is God's desire to promote your welfare to its highest good; to lead you to your ultimate growth.

Then say: *"I now call on this Power in faith and in love, asking it to heal me and make me perfectly whole."* Pause. Think about the meaning of your words. Then call: *"God, my Father, spirit of all love, all good, please make me well and whole."* Pause again and think about the meaning of your words. Remember God is the Spirit of Love which created the universe and man. Surely it can create a new cell, reduce a fever or adjust any part of the human mechanism to perfect working order. Moreover, it *desires to do so because it loves you.*

Finally say, *"I am being healed through the power of love and I am grateful that this is so."*

Then during the day bring every thought, word, act and desire within the law of love. Many, many times during the day repeat, "I am being healed through the power of love and I am grateful that this is so." This is not to impress God or the power of love that is doing the work. It is to impress your own consciousness, to keep you constantly aware of God's love for you. It is to keep your own mind up to that level of understanding and belief required for the healing to take place. If you change your high state of consciousness for a lower one of fear, doubt, impatience or worry then your healing will slow down or stop.

At night before you fall asleep review your day. Have you given way to words of hate, anger, fear or doubt? If so forgive yourself and ask God to forgive you. Then realize the past has been erased, vow to do better on the morrow and go to sleep feeling that Love has erased every mark against you and that your sins (mistakes) will be remembered no more.

Be sure to give thanks for your constant improvement in health whether you can see the improvement or not. Improvement is there, long before your physical senses can become aware of it.

If you are being attended by a physician be sure to give him your fullest co-operation and gratitude. Have faith in his competence and in his earnest desire to help you. He deserves your praise, and he needs your free-will co-operation if he is to serve you to the best of his ability. Be considerate. Don't be demanding, critical or fearful. Your doctor is a child of God and a servant unto Him. Anyone who will devote his life to helping suffering humanity, to abolishing pain and rebuilding bodies, is a servant of the Lord and worth our time, our prayers, our praise and our money. To appreciate your physician's efforts is in no way to relinquish your belief in the power of God's love to heal you. Far from it. It is rather to see your physician as a channel through which God can work. There are many levels of healing. Medicine is one of them. Be grateful for help from whatever source it may come. But remember at all times that the power of prayer still is the highest, best and quickest means of healing. But if you have not yet learned how to work on that level then work on another and thank God for all who help you.

If you are in a hospital, you have an excellent opportunity to work with love in its effort to bring about your healing. You can spend waking hours silently surrendering your heart to love, silently speaking, thinking and listening with love. You can bless the institution which was organized by love and is maintained by it.

Few hospitals ever pay their way. They are maintained by people who fervently care about their fellowmen and desire to help them. I am so keenly aware of this fact that I cannot walk down a hospital corridor without feeling that impact of love. It always brings the tears to my eyes and as the song has it, puts my heart on its knees just to know that there is so much love at work in the world.

Remember your nurses love their work, love to serve, or they wouldn't be there. *Bless* them! Be grateful for them. Let your gratitude and love show in your eyes, in your voice and in your treatment of them. Remember them with a little gift, no matter how small, as an extra token of love. And do *love them.* It is this warm feeling about all life and people, this outpouring of gratitude and of love, this earnest desire to promote the welfare of others, to share life and love with them, to see the highest good in them, that heals and restores one's own health as well as one's soul. I have known and worked with a great many welfare and charity patients of one kind or another, and the sad truth is that almost without an exception, they were ungrateful, unhappy, demanding, and critical people. One woman who had been supported by the County and various State aids for more than fifteen years had no good word to say to anyone nor about anyone. I once asked her by what right she demanded for her support the tax money of fine, struggling young people who were rearing a family, owed her nothing, and remained unknown to her. "Why should strangers pay your bills?" I demanded to know. The thought was so new to her that it required several days for her to think it over. It stirred up so much within her that her pride eventually lifted her out of the state of

blaming everyone except herself for the condition she
had so long endured.

Wherever you are when you are ill, let your mind
often go out into space. Think of the beautiful world
around you, of the perfect law and order in evidence
everywhere. Realize you are not alone. God is not unaware of you. Think of the long history of the human
race on earth. Remember that nothing ever has defeated it. Know that nothing can. In this way, still all
your fears of the future, fears about your loved ones,
fears about eternity.

Stop all idle or active fears about death. Death is a
door which opens to let us pass into a new way of life.
Since all existence is a forward movement, then the life
after death must necessarily be a better one than the
one we lead here. And if you love, greatly desire, life
then you can live on, forever, no matter how many
changes and adjustments you may have to make before
you are able to let Christ Consciousness rule in your
life. Your illness is a temporary thing. *Life is eternal.*
Your stay on earth is at most an ephemeral visit, but
your existence is eternal if you so desire it. Think then,
on the eternal things, and you will find that through
the law of love, the temporary ones are healed.

Are you ill? My friend, love can heal you. Go back
in memory to the happiest, the most love-filled days of
your life, back to childhood if necessary. Recapture the
mood of those days when you felt secure and happy
knowing you were loved. Become again in thought and
feeling as a little child. Relax and remember that you
are a child of Father time and Mother nature. Then go
a little higher in consciousness and realize there is a
great sustaining power in the universe which loves you

far more than you have ever loved anything in all your life. All we know of love is but a spark, a reflection of that love. That great Love now holds you tenderly, knows what is happening to you, and will take care of you.

When you feel too tired or too ill to think straight, or to repeat affirmations, relax, smile to yourself, and feel the very love of God enfolding you, desiring all good for you. If the hour comes when you know you are to walk through the valley of the shadow of death, still you need fear no evil. For love is ever with you. Trust love to see you through this world and all worlds to come. Listen with love my friend, and you will hear the Voice of God saying, "Come home, oh weary child, come home."

CHAPTER NINE

To Develop Your Talent

SOME of the most pitiful problems that have come to my attention were those of people no longer young who had suddenly realized that their failure in life and their deep unhappiness were their own fault. They believed that they could have been a great success—if they had only developed their talent instead of burying it!

Why do people bury their talent? Because they do not love it enough, set no real value on it or have no ambition, no willingness to work with God. They do not love life.

Webster defines talent as a "pre-eminent and special aptitude; faculty for effective performance along certain lines. Superior intelligence and ability as for business or artistic pursuits."

All people are born with a talent, a special aptitude to handle the stuff of life. We each have a very special job to do which we can do better than any other work and better than any one else can do it. No matter what else we do with life, we never are completely happy unless and until we develop our share of God. We are not happy because we are not whole even though we may have earned a good and honest living, served the world and even acquired a fortune. Our talent was given us to love so much that we would work with it and by doing so, learn more about God, ourselves and our fellowmen than in any other way.

There is another side, another meaning to developing one's talent. Jesus devoted a whole parable to what happens when we fail to multiply by use that which we have and are. Simplified, it is the parable of the man who trusted his servants with talents while he was away. One hid his talent. The others put theirs to use and multiplied them. On his return, the man required an accounting of his servants. Those who had multiplied their talents were called good and faithful servants, the one who had hidden his one talent was rebuked and his one talent was taken from him and given to the man who now had ten talents. The parable is found in the 25th chapter of *Matthew* from the 14th verse on and should be read by those who desire to develop fully their own talent.

In Jesus' parable the surface meaning of the word talent is money. But money is a symbol. Money is not reality. The realities are principles and not things. So in reading the parable we must look for the below-surface meanings. Bible passages have been found to have several meanings depending upon whether they apply to the mental, physical or spiritual plane. The talent in Jesus' parable means a measure or unit of life; an individual unit of consciousness or selfhood. In our modern world a talent is a symbol of money, for if put to use, it earns money.

Here is the soul of the Bible parable: "For unto everyone that hath shall be given, and he shall have abundance; but from him that hath not shall be taken away even that which he hath." (*Matthew* 25:29)

Considered in the light of all else Jesus taught we see the inexorable law in that passage. It says that unless we grow by multiplying our original measure of life, we shall cease to be as an individual. We must of ourselves either multiply that which we are or become extinct as the result of having our original measure of existence "taken away" by law. God cannot increase ourselves for us because we have free will. Multiply, or be cast "into outer darkness," the great void which has neither Light, individuality, nor consciousness of its own. Multiply by use or your measure of being will revert to a static condition upon which others who have multiplied themselves may draw. In shorter words, *love life, use it under the law of love, or perish.*

By using life we not only multiply that which we were but we receive additional abundance of life from the total of all there is. This is natural. By our work we produce more of life than there was and so we have more on which to draw. By multiplying our own unit of being we draw to ourselves the "buried" or unused units of those who refuse to multiply or evolve. A crude comparison is that of a grain of wheat cast into the earth which has the power to germinate but does not do so and therefore decays, becoming part of the soil food for the grain next to it which is alive and growing—multiplying its share of life.

By working with God we are "good and faithful servants," and so we "enter into the joy of our Lord." This joy is a two-fold one and operates on two levels. By using what we are, we multiply that measure of existence, no matter how small our understanding of God and Life may be. Soon we find ourselves mastering many things. The more we understand, the more we are able to use, command and develop on larger and larger scales. This is true of our every day work-talents also.

Our talent need not be a big five-point one in order to come under the law. We find in verse 34 through 40 of *Matthew* 25, that the good, those who are to inherit

the kingdom "prepared . . . from the foundation of
the world," are those who loved and served their fellowmen; who have fed the hungry, clothed the naked, and
ministered to the sick and imprisoned. There are many
levels of hunger, sickness and imprisonment. To follow
through with all the hidden meanings of those six verses
would need a volume in itself and require a study of
all Jesus said and did. We must hasten on to the conclusion: the Lord says, "Inasmuch as ye have done it
unto the least of these ye have done it unto me." All
Jesus' teachings go to prove that as *we do unto others we
do unto God, our fellowmen and ourselves.*

Serve in love or perish. That is the nature of the universe, the law of existence, the Will of God, the way
evolution has worked since God gave man free will.
This is both the ultimatum and the promise. If we work
in love, we multiply ourselves and we shall eventually
find God, joy and eternal life, creating them for ourselves by our *own willingness, our own efforts, our love.*

But the Great Creative Spirit of the Universe, our
God, is indeed the intent of love and justice itself beyond the present capacity of feeble mortal minds to
understand. Nor do we need to understand at this time.
We have eternity in which to cope with such facts. We
are not held accountable until we understand as did the
servant who had only one talent. He understood, but he
decided to bury his talent rather than put it to use.
God Himself cannot keep us in existence if we choose
to refuse life.

In this parable Jesus was telling us about the laws of
existence. We should listen and take heed for He knew
more about the laws than any man who has lived before
or since. Too many people have the old idea of my-
thology in worship. Too long the world has looked upon
Jesus as a far-off Divine Being, a very Son of God whom

no mere mortal could hope to emulate. This is not what Jesus taught. He called Himself the "son of man" and said that anyone could do that which He did when they learned the laws and how to work with them. This is the view which science will take, already has taken it seems to me, and which may yet do more to save man from destroying himself than the old ideas of worshiping God have been able to do.

We are now ready to look at some of the lower levels of talent at work. But we should keep in mind that it is by our lower level talents that we reach the higher level as related in the parable.

A minister who was sad and failing in his profession confessed to me that he had long wanted to open a garage and work as an automobile mechanic. I told him to do so. For some reason he could communicate with God and understand the universe better in the exactness of the mechanic's trade than he could in preaching the Gospel. He said "the hum of a perfectly tuned up motor sounded better to his ears than a church hymn."

But the man lacked the courage to break his established thinking about life. I often wonder what that man would have discovered, what he might have given the world if he had had the courage to take off his ministerial robe, put on the mechanic's overall and go to work with God at a job he *loved*. He cared so much about his real talent that he used to sit at his study window and listen to the cars go by on the boulevard mentally checking "what was wrong with them by the sounds they made." The happiest hours of his life were spent working with his car, going through books about motors. His ministerial duties were mere habits performed from a sense of duty, and a fear of appearing a failure. But he had buried his talent.

A surgeon told me he had never wanted to study

medicine but that it had been impressed upon him from early childhood that he "must become a doctor" and so he dutifully became one. It ruined his health and his happiness. He said he felt he had only worked and "never lived at all." I advised him to resign while there was time but he did not, though he confessed he had added "little if anything to his profession or to the field of medicine in any way." He had always wanted to be a farmer. The joy of his life, the one thing he really loved was his occasional stolen visit to the country, where he would rise before daybreak. At that hour he "felt he could live forever; that there was something all around him alive, working in the air and in the very soil." He was conscious of being urged to work with it though he never once dared to "risk his hands." Here was a work he loved and only God knows what this man might have discovered had he followed his natural faculties, his natural aptitudes. But as a child he had been wretchedly poor, he said. His parents, having suffered through poverty, convinced him there was "no money in farming; nothing but hard work," and he had believed them.

The truth is that when we work at our God-given task, it is not a burdensome toil but the greatest of joys, for our inner Lord is pleased when we are about our Father's business. Love ever makes life a joy, not a burden. When we apply ourselves to the job God has selected us to do we are working with Him and we inwardly know that we cannot fail.

Even more tragic are those people who recognized their talent, tried to develop it but through misunderstanding the laws of love or refusal to live within them, became frustrated failures. Here is one example:

A certain young man now thirty looks years older and

finished with life. When he was eighteen, he was headed for a career as a singer. He had everything he needed to go with his glorious voice except the right attitude toward people. His teachers did not long tolerate his abusive temper and his acid criticism. Nor did his friends. He failed before he got started. That attitude would have ruined his voice sooner or later in any case. Today he is a clerk in a grocery store. He spends his money for recordings of some of the very same "little voices" he used to laugh at.

On the other hand, the possessors of those "little voices" loved and appreciated their talent so much that they put it out to use and along with it, loved people, their audience and life. They had more than just a voice box in their throat. They had the intangibles of willingness to serve, desire to please, appreciation of praise and of others. They never forgot that their goal, even when they were very far from it, was to sing to people. One of the singers who once cringed under the sharp words of the grocery clerk explained his success to me in this way: "I knew I had a small voice so I figured I'd have to develop a very large personality. I had to make the people love me enough to overlook the smallness of my voice. And I had to be so sincere about it that my sincerity would carry over to them before I ever opened my mouth. I did the trick by learning to love people."

That is true of all talents which take one before the public. It is especially true of radio performers of all kinds. A man who had been on the radio for sixteen years told me he early discovered the fact that the microphone has an uncanny way of picking up and amplifying the slightest tone of insincerity just as it enlarges the one that is sincere.

To try to develop a talent in a spiritually illegal manner is to bury it. Every criminal I ever worked with had a talent which he had been using against himself, his own life and his soul although he thought of it as "pitting his wits against the world and sometimes winning." Only a fool imagines he can cheat nature, outwit God. Can man the *created* be greater or know more than God, the *Creator?* I have helped several gambling addicts to perfect healing by helping them to learn how to develop their real talent under the law of love.

Developing our talent means for most of us what it meant for Jenny, putting our special ability, our aptitude, our little one-point talent to work in some commercial pursuit which appeals to us and by which we can earn a living.

But even here we cannot overlook the law of love, the desire for good and the willingness to promote the welfare of all. The man building a commercial enterprise on anything less than all truth, honesty, love of goodness, self and brother is building to an eventual fall. For all not built by the Father will have to be torn down and built anew.

Poverty will vanish from the face of the earth when mankind as a whole stops trying to "get a bargain," or "something for nothing," from his fellowmen. God does not cheat one man in order to enrich another, nor does He allow us to do so. The man who takes an undue profit out of his laborer's goods or services, steals from himself materially and spiritually. He has buried his talent. He has refused to put himself out for the honest use of God and his fellowmen.

Now what about you and your talent? If you have one already at work you need but obey the rules. Accept once and for all that you can develop it or you would not have been given the task in the first place. Your ambition is equal to your ability to deliver. Your purchasing power is equal to your needs. When you work at your talent through love, you have signed up with the creative power of the universe as manager and copartner. But the first move is yours, always. "God helps those who help themselves," surely applies to developing one's talent.

There is a creative spirit waiting for you to call upon it. Say, *"I love my talent and my talent loves me,"* as you train for or work at your task. Say, *"I love God and God loves me."* Also, *"I love people and people love me."* If working at your talent sometimes seems to take too many hours, remember that time is not being wasted. "I am multiplying my life through love; I am multiplying my talent through love," often repeated will refresh and restore you.

Once you have "arrived" and are actually performing on the job whether it is the smallest task or the biggest in the nation, keep yourself aware of the force of love by saying *"I work for God's people and God's people work for me."* It cannot be otherwise. All the money you will ever earn by putting your talent to work will come to you through the hands of others.

Whatever your work, do it well. As you do unto others you are doing unto yourself and to God. If it is not your own beloved talent, then work toward that day when you will be giving all your time to your talent, but do not slight the task at hand. Take the attitude that the work you are doing now if good and honest, will lead to an opening for working at your talent and remember your prayer program for that opening.

At this point someone is pretty sure to say, "But how can I? I'm only a housewife," or "I'm a husband with a family to feed "

Listen, my friends, if you really know what your talent is and if you love it so much that you'd pay for the privilege of working at it because there was no other way to get a chance to perform, then never doubt that you'll develop that talent. The only reason you have not already done so is that some mental block exists in your own mind to prevent this development. The talent is the very call of God to go to work for Him. Who or what can stand against you when you start to work with God? As for being a busy housewife with no time to do the extra job God has assigned you to do, I'd like to point out that being a mother or a good wife to a good man is job enough. Also, I'd like to mention the fact that the world's most successful women, those who have given most to their fellowmen have been mothers along with their other jobs. A talent is no load to carry. It is the star that leads on and on, making all other loads lighter. It is a promise of God. Do your part and God will do His, never fear. Remember, God will benefit by your success.

Remember too, that you have the weight, opinion and love of the world back of you, rooting for you. Whether you stop to think about it or not, the world shares in your success. All people wish to be in better circumstances. When you have succeeded with your talent, some of the good flows out to the world in ever widening circles. Every man gets an unearned benefit by the other man's success. Don't let temporary petty jealousies disturb you. Don't let the fearful little minds of uninformed persons tell you it can't be done. Pay no attention at all to well meaning but misguided relatives who try to run your life. I once advised a young man to leave home for this very reason. His parents, who would gladly have choked me at the time, are today busy singing my praises and bragging about their son who has made such a wonderful success. Relatives are the grave diggers of more buried talents than they ever dream of. The guilt is twofold. It rests with the one who lets his talent be buried alive and with the one who compels its interment.

Listen only to your own Soul and to God. Go straight to the great collective Christ Mind of the world for help. That highest self in each man is there, separated from personalities, wishing you success, ready and able to help you by its good desire, its love. Recognize that aid. Trust it fully. Call on it and you will get help from it. I know a lawyer who never takes a case to court without first meditating alone, calling on this collective wisdom and good, on God, for guidance. He seldom loses a case. He has refused to take a good many because he felt they were against the law of love. He desires always to work with God, and to avoid the "stupidity of ever trying to break a spiritual law or trying to work against God."

"But how am I to know what my talent is?" someone may say. "Your talent is the thing you *love to do,* the thing that you get excited about, that urges you to get into action," is the answer. If you don't know what your talent is, ask yourself! Watch yourself all day for weeks, months if need be. What really interests you? Don't pretend. Don't hide. Don't be falsely modest nor too self-critical. Still don't know? Well, try this:

Ask God to show you. Go to your meditation room. Assume the attitude of a trusting little child. Say, "Father, I know you have given me a work to do for Thee, myself and my fellowmen. I am willing and anxious to do that work. But I do not see clearly what it is. Please show me my talent and how to go about developing it."

Pause, wait and again assume the attitude of a little child. *Expect an answer.* If it does not come at once go right on assuming that the answer has come. For it has. It came to earth with you. Your earth ears are not yet tuned to hear the voice of God. But they will be if you persist in the belief that they are. Continue your efforts, and one day the answer will come so clearly to your mind you will wonder why you did not think of that before. We see how this law works on the physical plane. From a brilliantly lighted room we step into a dark one and at first we "can't see a thing," but presently, when our physical eyes have become adjusted to the darkness, we can easily make out objects in the room.

Start to work with your talent. See it as a labor of love. Look with the eyes of love at it, at your fellowmen and at all nature. Speak and listen with love. Think with the mind of love. Soon you will hear the voice of God saying, "Come up higher." And you will double, treble your efforts and your output. Eventually you will discover that to work with God is to be sure of success. All worry about the future, all speculation about the outcome of your efforts, your ability, will be dissolved in the warmth and sureness of love. For if you love life, you love your talent. And where love is, there is success also, whether with the temporary task of earning your bread and butter, or your great work, the work of developing your measure of being, your Soul. *Love never fails.*

Add to your notes:

"I work with love and love works with me. I do not fail love and love never fails me."

PART FOUR

How to Trust the Spirit of Love

CHAPTER TEN

To Help Your Loved Ones

"MY LIFE would be all right if only I could do something to help" my loved one, is the cry of many. Others say, "How can I make" my loved one do this or that.

If we are looking for happiness and are convinced it can come to us only if some other person changes his way of life, reforms, treats us differently, lives after our pattern, we might as well give up. We have no moral right to "make people over." God has decreed that each man has a right to find perfection and peace, Divine Love, in his own way even if he makes mistakes and harms himself in doing so.

We cannot too often remember that beyond a certain point we dare not try to handle other people's lives. Our free will does not give us the authority to overcome our brother's free will. Our powers of exercising our free will end exactly at the spot where his begins. When we cross that line, we are taking liberties with another human soul which God Himself does not presume to do. Like Jesus we should teach, demonstrate according to the law of love, set an example, help when called upon but never try to usurp. This does not mean that we should not try to train young children of course.

When we feel the urge to "lay down the law" to someone dear to us or to someone who we feel is on the wrong path, we should pause and ask ourselves why do we so want to tell them what to do and how to do it.

"Because," comes the answer (and rather heatedly more likely than not) "we do love them and we therefore know what is best for them."

What manner of love is this? The love that Christ Jesus showed and said we should have for each other? Paul's love, that "seeketh not its own, is long suffering and kind"? Or is it a mixture of fear, a desire to fulfill the frustration in our own lives by dominating the life of another? Is it a downright distrust of God's ability and intention to handle the problem involved? We must get our reasoning straight before we can hope truly to help another.

"My way because it is best for you," can become "my way or die." No one is so perfect in love that he is capable of dominating the life of another. Free will is the gift of God. Any attempt to overcome it, imprison it in falsehoods, subdue and mislead it wilfully for a selfish or evil purpose is a crime against man and an attempt to mock God. Any attempt to do it through good intentions is a distrust of the spirit of love, God, and shows lack of faith, wisdom and love.

Past wars between nations and between groups grew out of one interest trying to force its will upon another. Church and State have been equally guilty. This domination always fails eventually. Revolution overthrows tryants forever because every man knows with an inherent wisdom that he was born free and has a right and a divine duty to exercise his will. Thus children leave parents to start out for themselves. All of us resent unfair criticism and bondage, dislike being ordered about and grow restive under restrictions. In the final analysis the Soul is ashamed and we are irritated when we let another direct our lives, for we know it is our duty and privilege to direct them ourselves.

How can we be sure our desire to help our loved one is motivated by good, by the very spirit of love and not merely by our own fear or domination at work? There is one unfailing test: are we unselfishly willing to pray as earnestly for the failure of our plan if it should not develop for the loved one's highest good, as we are to pray for its success if it is in his best interests? Are we willing to admit that it is entirely possible that our way is entirely wrong? If we are willing to leave the matter up to the Divine Mind for judging then we can be sure we are honestly desirous of helping the loved one for his own good.

But how shall we act, once sure our desire is right?

The way to help a loved one overcome his faults, find happiness, maintain and restore health, overcome any kind of problem and be guided in any undertaking is to *trust the spirit or intent of love and to work with it instead of against it.* Love, we must remember is the force which creates good and only good. And it always creates more good than existed before it set to work to promote the welfare of the beloved.

The following example covers all the points of the procedure as I have successfully used it with others, regardless of what the person's problem may have been. It works equally well for healing gambling, drinking, broken homes, and misunderstandings of all kinds. The key words in it are italicized for the reader's after study.

A man came to me greatly disturbed about his son who was "breaking the hearts" of those who loved him. He was especially breaking the heart of his young wife whom the whole family loved. The son always had been "a little restless, different from the other members of the family." He was critical. In school he had been ambitious and had bitterly resented his parent's poverty which he felt prevented him from going to college. When his father pointed out the fact that thousands of fine young men worked their way through college the son was angry. He was the youngest member of the family. "Seems like Bill always wanted more than the others; never was satisfied with our lot in life."

The family long had been church members, but the young man "scoffed at it all," saying it had done them no good; had not improved their position in life. About two years before, the young man had married and was now the father of a baby son.

"Bill's grown so much worse since the baby came," said the father. "I can't understand Bill. He loves the baby and his wife. I get so exasperated with him I could shake him."

With all the facts finally before me I said, "Bill is in open revolt against his present way of life, poverty and hard work. He, like most of the members of his generation, has been brought up on ideas of 'getting something better.' The sellers of wares never let up on stimulating a prospective customer to buy, and they start out on the kindergarten group. Unless we know how to handle such stimulation and see our desires as a natural part of the law of progressive growth, refusing to be unduly urged, we are too likely to fall into the ditch where Bill has fallen. It is not Bill's *desire for things* of life which is causing the trouble, but the fact that *he sees no way to acquire them*. He knows nothing about his own inner powers which if developed would bring him the things. His purpose is right. His discontent is divine. His idea of how to achieve what he desires for his wife, his child and himself is wrong. That is what we must heal."

The young man had lately taken to "running around with some Communistic talking friends and accepting their ideas as a way of improving their own fortunes." Greatly disturbed the father said, "How can we make the boy see—"

I said "In effect you are saying, 'Now God, I know you are pretty wonderful at solving most problems but when it comes to my son Bill you're just not big enough. You'd better let me handle this,' " and after a while the man admitted that he had been thinking prayer would do no good.

"We can't make your son see what is right," I said. "But his own Christ Mind can remind him, present the true facts to him so clearly that he will see for himself what to do. He will then look to the universal spirit of love for help and not to men. He will then leave his ideas of force as spiritually illegal and will start to trust and to work with his desires within the law of all good for all men."

"But where do I come in?" the father worried.

"By trusting the power of love and by working with it," I replied. "This means that we are to bring *our own desires, acts, and belief on behalf of Bill within the law of love.* We are going to work with principles and not with Bill. If you actually believe there is a power higher than the power of God, the very Spirit of love and all good, then there is no use to try to work for your son. You will not help him. You will hinder him. But if you can accept as truth beyond all doubt and fear that there is a spirit of love throughout the universe which always has protected man in the past and always will aid all who call upon it, then you can help your son. Our first step in helping your son is to agree on that point. Can you agree?"

After a long time of talking, after much study on the man's part and as he said, "revising considerable of his former ideas on the subject so that he would be sure he had stopped telling God what to do," the man came to the point of agreement. We then set to work with the process I mentioned in Jenny's story, that of placing a circle of love around the loved one. And this is how we did it. To the father I said:

"We shall form a *circle of love*. It will be composed of our thoughts, feelings, desires, hopes, and positive knowledge of what is right for Bill. It will be *intelligent, alive,* and it *will grow*. It will be creative for it is made of the same power which created man. It will come from our mind and heart, made up of our love of all good and will include our honest desire to promote the welfare of Bill in such a way that it promotes the welfare of all other men as well. It will be made up of the best we have and know in our own lives. We shall then place that circle of living love around Bill by our projected desire for his good. We shall set it into motion by our spoken word. Our word shall not return unto us void but it will accomplish that which we desire it to do. Our word, being creative, will create after its kind."

To all this the father desired to agree and we worked back and forth with our thoughts about it until we could and did agree on all the points concerned. We then placed the circle by saying, "We have now placed a circle of love around you, Bill. No harm can come to you through it. No harm can go through it from you to another. For love rules your life."

I further instructed: "Inside that circle we must see

Bill as he goes about his daily work. And back of him we shall see his own Christ Self, the man who he will eventually be when he has lived long enough and evolved toward Truth, or things as they are. We see back of him, towering above his small present mortal self, that purified man, the man who has been born again, in Christ, the man in whom the Adam man has died and the Christ man been born."

On all this we agreed.

"Now as your son goes about his daily life we see speaking to him and guiding him, this Christ Self which we must always remember is the pattern of perfection toward which all men are striving. We hear the Divine in your son speaking to the mortal in him. We see the mortal man listening. We see him turning from his way of fear and frustration to the way of love, truth, beauty, and righteousness. We see him turning to the paths of peace and plenty. We see him making his outer world after that inner perfect pattern. We see him doing this by *bringing his every desire, act and belief under the law of progressive good for all men including himself.*"

On all this we agreed, and we talked at great length about the reason our words were truth. I was trying to help the father bring his own consciousness up to the level of seeing truth. To the reader unfamiliar with Truth or the New Thought interpretation of Jesus' teachings, this may seem a far-fetched, involved or even mysterious method of helping a loved one. But the more advanced student will recognize it as Christ's method of teaching by parables. If the sufferer already knew how to use the principle he would not be coming for help. I find I cannot help until I can raise the level of the understanding of the student to a point where he can grasp the principle. There may be a much better

way of accomplishing this than I have found, but to
date I find the picture method works best. And this is
just as true for the intelligent and well educated as
it was for Jenny. Her whole life was made over by just
such a portrayal of principles. It does take a great deal
of time, patience and repeated effort, but once the
student mentally grasps the law through pictures, it
is his for life, and he can then use it at will. So it is worth
while no matter how long it takes to teach him.

If that father had continued to argue with his son,
Bill would have gone more deeply into his own devices
for he already had lost all respect for his father's way
of life as a means of accomplishing the material things
he desired. Yet he had within himself that higher self,
the Christ Consciousness. In working with Bill silently,
we did not need his consent for we kept within his rights
of free will. We did this by going above it, going directly
to the highest law, God. That we always have the right
and the duty to do.

As the father and I worked in prayer for Bill, the
father explained to his family as best he could what
we were trying to do. They joined in. Soon after we
had started to work, Bill said to his wife, "What's happened to you? You don't quarrel at me any more."

"Because I love you as you are," said his wife, meaning
his inner self, and not the frustrated, puzzled fighting
outer self.

Before long the young man noticed that none of the
family criticized him, none blamed him. He did not
know they were deliberately not seeing, not asking, not
even advising him about his previous faults and attitudes in spite of the fact that for a time those faults continued. With no one to argue with at home, the boy
soon grew quieter. He could not do otherwise in that

living, growing, glowing circle of love around him! All contention in the family, all fear, resentment and argument ceased. They were *behaving as if they already had received the answer to their prayers about Bill.*

One day Bill told his father he had an offer of a new job. He took it, left his labor union, stopped seeing his hotheaded Communist friends and before long stopped telling his father he was wrong about everything. A little later, he went into a small business venture for himself. After that he made progress by leaps and bounds. One success brings another when we work with love. It is part of our study of the law of love to see how and why he succeeded.

Going into business for himself restored his soul and righted his attitude toward others since he had righted it toward himself. He began to build up self-confidence and self-pride of a good kind. He no longer felt secretly impotent and worthless. He was at last fulfilling the commandment to "love thyself." When we began to see worth in Bill we helped him to see worth in himself, to trust and work with love. Then it was not long before others began to see worth in Bill also. Through this avenue of love he was able to acquire a small home with a very modest down payment. An elderly couple "trusted him because they saw he had such faith in himself and was so devoted to his family." They sold him the little place they no longer needed. Their faith in him made a profound impression on the young man. By seeing the worth in others and the essence of their intent to do good, he began to trust love.

With the acquisition of that little home the change in Bill was simply astounding. He now had pride of ownership where he once had had shame of poverty. He loved his home and desired to promote this good. His whole attitude of destroying in order to receive, curbing others in order to gain for himself, changed to ways of constructive living through love. He now saw the necessity and desirability of protecting others and helping them to grow and to create. This new feeling about all life, all men and the very nature of things or God, began with loving himself. He no longer had to pretend he hated "conditions" for he now knew a way to change conditions. With one real accomplishment to his credit his faith increased tremendously.

One day when we felt Bill was well enough along with his new way of life, his father told him about our work. Bill confessed he had felt the effect of that circle as something "warm and safe around him that made him think in a way he never had thought before." He began to "feel unafraid; to see he was going to solve his problems." One day he said, "Dad, you're a better Christian than I thought you were." This amazed his father who thought Bill had renounced church and religion while all the time, he was actually looking for something more than he had found in religion so far. Bill did not go back to his old way. He had turned within for a power that always had been there waiting to be called upon.

When we learn to take our desires to the creative power of the universe, we do not feel the need of clubs in hand, the organized force of men. For we find love, the desire for good for all to be the greatest power of all. We discover the fact that our desire was implanted in us so that we would make an effort to satisfy it and by that effort, grow. We learn eventually to trust love. But how much better it would be and how much faster we'd travel if we set out by trusting love in the first place!

To help your loved one there is only one thing you can do in safety and that is to *help him become aware of his own inner power.* He does not have to rely on your power. You assert your influence by raising your own consciousness of love, by trusting it farther than you can possibly see, to guide, protect and help that loved one.

The best way to keep "hands off" and let love do the work is to place that living, growing, glowing circle of love around him. The more visual and real you can make it in your own mind, the more quickly you will raise the level of your consciousness. Give your circle of love a color. I prefer gold for it is easily seen. See your circle composed of tiny particles as of mist or fog. See it ever spreading out and around your loved one. If you are trying to bring a loved one home as was Jenny, then place yourself in the center of the circle. See it as expanding into an ever larger circle of love, ever alive and growing until it encompasses the world if necessary. Then know that it will find that loved one and begin by love, not will power or force, to draw him to you.

In using the circle for the uplift and protection of a loved one, you must see him inside the circle, being talked to by his highest self rather than by you. Never picture yourself or anyone else as using force with your loved one.

If you will use the circle of living love to help your loved one you will find your worries and fears about him will fall from you like a discarded cloak. You need to liberate him. Your apprehensions and scoldings will hold him down exactly as if you had submerged him in water. As long as you fear for him, you are setting forces into motion to make those fears come true, after their kind.

When you rise in your own consciousness and really trust love, you broadcast that fact to him, for thoughts about a loved one are projected at a tremendous rate of vibration. You feel intently about him. Loving him, you cannot do otherwise. He is in tune with you even though he may seem to differ on all opinions about life and affairs. *He hears your belief.* He reacts to it. And the lower he is in estimation of himself the more he *will believe and react* to your most strongly held and projected opinions about him.

So do not criticize. Look with the eyes of love, listen and speak with love. Do not agonize about all the dreadful things that might happen, when he is on an airplane or automobile trip, for example. Bring all your thoughts about him under love. Bring all your desires, acts and faith under love. Do not look for the worst. Look for and believe in the best. Withdraw all thoughts, even your prayers, until you can begin to trust love. Let your prayer for yourself and your loved one be "God I thank thee for increased wisdom and love." Then you will be thinking about him with the mind of love. Then you will be trusting love, which means trusting God's earnest desire to promote the welfare of your loved one and of yourself as well.

It is when we trust God fully that we are able to build a circle composed of our thoughts, words and beliefs about love. In this way we go to the Father that is in our loved one, reminding him to go to the Father of us all. We thus urge his mortal self to listen to his Divine, immortal self.

If you are keeping notes and making use of the affirmations so far given, add this to them:

"God loves him, and he loves God. God speaks to

him and he listens. God directs, and he follows. And I am grateful that this is so."

In using it mention the name of your loved one. Then cast all sense of burden from your own mind and heart. You do not have to do the work. It is done for you.

CHAPTER ELEVEN

To Lead You to Paradise

"HERE we are next to the last chapter and you haven't yet mentioned *my* problem!"

Yes, my friend, I hear your cry. I hear you saying "If only I could—" and "If—, then I'd be the happiest person in the world!"

Your problem is the one faced by all human beings, the problem of finding God, and so, perfection. For our three basic urges to *live,* to *love* and to *learn* (desire for liberty) are but parts of a whole, the urge to find paradise, that heaven on earth which we have longed for all our individual lives and which mankind has sought from the beginning.

Because it led us to desires, acts and beliefs, this urge to find a perfect state of existence, God, and to learn the whole story of man has always led the human race forward. The struggle to satisfy the urge has taught and almost civilized man. What we so often forget is that we could never have created our desires ourselves. They were implanted in us by God so that we would do something about satisfying them. This is the voice of God saying "Come up higher." If we try to fulfill the urge we cannot fail. The weak link in our chain of growth is our fear, our lack of faith. That is what is wrong with you now, fear.

We are all like anxious little children at the railway station waiting to go to the country to visit grandparents who will shower us with love and happiness. We too, fear the train will never come, leaving us on the platform, defeated and unsatisfied. Or like Jenny, we feel safe as long as we can "pitch in and do things ourselves," but trusting an unseen power to lead us through life sometimes proves too much for us. When things go wrong with our plans, we are apt to give up our brave new project of changing our lives for the better and settle down, blame others, or make excuses for our failures, trying somehow to bear things as they are. We just can't believe there is Something interested in our welfare. We do not *trust* love.

In the early stages of our life-changing program we shall find it greatly helps to trust love by reminding ourselves that our very desire for a more perfect life is proof in itself that the Spirit is at work in us. Those poor souls who seem to be sleep-walking through life never lift their eyes to the stars, never ask a question of God, know no discontent. Their existence is as yet only a little higher than that of a turnip or a turtle. So if you are discontent you can be sure the Spirit of the eternal is working in you. Be glad! It is trying to quicken you to an awareness of more truth, more beauty, more love. When you become aware of them your next step will be to acquire them, make them part of your life. Those who are seeking something better are on the way to finding it. Persist!

There is great hope for you if you see wrongs that need to be righted, if you feel the need of more truth and beauty. So dry your eyes. Start over. Look around you at others who are successful. Rejoice in their good. Say, *"I have a deathless, sleepless Spirit within me which is leading me on to higher good. I cannot fail! My discontent is Divine."*

Then when you begin to see a little progress, your joy of achievement will carry you forward to new desires. When these are attained, they will carry you on still higher. This pattern of desire fulfilled, new desire born, will endlessly repeat itself in the growing Soul.

Then what? After we have met all the requirements as before set forth and have completely changed our lives through love, do we eventually find a state of eternal bliss on earth, of complete satisfaction? Or do we find that our new and abundant prosperity, our health, our talent employed in a work we love doing, our friends, peace and love still do not fill all the vacancies in our lives? The answer is, we find with a shock that there still is something lacking. And the more we succeed in our individual lives by using the power of love, the more we become aware of a gnawing hidden spiritual hunger. Is it good and something to be encouraged, or bad and something to be overcome? How can we use this fact to further our hopes for paradise?

Christ Jesus knew this same feeling and was often wearied in spirit. He sometimes sighed deeply within himself and had to go into the desert to rest. Therefore, we should see this feeling as good. It is Divine discontent. We should listen to this uneasiness of our Soul. It is God inviting us to learn and to increase. It is the spirit of love reminding us that struggles are natural and useful, that by them we go forward, that life is eternal, that we should never become content on earth lest we fall asleep and cease to grow. It is God reminding us that we should desire more and more of life, not merely of things. Our Souls are unlimited. This discontent is proof that we have not used all our powers; that a vast storehouse lies yet to be tapped. It is the aching of spiritual muscles asking to be used.

There is yet another side to this Divine discontent. It is God inviting us to make a heaven on earth for all men as well as for ourselves and warning us that our individual heaven is in danger as long as there is hell all around us in which our fellowmen live. We come at last to a place where we greatly desire to help all men to learn our new way of life. We suffer keenly seeing individuals and whole nations of men hurt themselves, living in poverty, and making mistakes while all the time it is possible for them to rise in consciousness and go to the Father.

We need not be radiantly happy every second of our lives. Happiness is often a result of contrasts and comparisons. We should accept the fact that there is no perfect escape from this Divine discontent in the present state of the human race's development. For all our senses remind us of paradise, or the possibility of creating a perfect state. We gaze upon a gold and rose sunset above a silver sea. The beauty and peace of it are not pure pleasure, for beauty, a measure of perfection, always makes us a little sad in whatever form we may happen to behold her. This sadness is a kind of homesickness for our natural state or rightful home. It is looking backward to remember with our Christ mind the time "before Abraham was," and looking forward to heaven on earth with our mortal mind to see so much that must be done. Back of this sadness is of course an unconscious fear that we shall not be able to measure up to God's confidence in our ability. *The remedy is to trust our powers more fully.* Love never fails. And this is love at work.

We need not grow too discouraged in facing the long

hard road ahead of humanity. We can at any time turn quickly to beauty, to measures of pure harmony and so restore our soul. We can look at the stars, walk in the country, work in the garden, play with children, watch love at work and be reminded of God. However, it is to the harmony of music that many of us owe our most vivid glimpses of paradise, our most poignant discontent with things as they are, our most ardent plans and hopes to achieve our paradise, our greatest revitalizer for the day's labor at hand.

I have often used music to refill my soul-self after long draining hours of trying to help some poor soul who was struggling to understand truth. It is a method I strongly recommend to all who are trying to build up a consciousness of love and an increased faith in the possibility of heaven on earth. Here is an example of what I mean:

Recently we sat at night under the stars listening to soul-stirring music in Hollywood Bowl. There we were, several thousand people, strangers for the most part, but, I observed, blood kin in our common hunger for beauty and harmony. This was the spirit of love at work.

I looked around at their faces, wrapped in the semi-darkness. I watched their expressions as the harmonies carried them on to beauty. The music came in full flowing tones, deep and wide, like the troubles of man. Their faces were sad with remembering. Problems sat heavily upon them. Then there came the clear small voice of the flutes, lifted high above the subdued tones, like a promise of a new and better way of life for sorrowing mankind. Then I saw hope in their faces, a new belief that their desire to create paradise, to promote

the welfare of all men, to create heaven on earth, could
be realized.

I sat silently weeping in joy, seeing once again that
all men are brothers, all bound together in the love of
God their creator, all safe in His desire for their welfare. I saw again that in time men will stop their wars
and crimes, their lust and greed and will give up their
hates and fears to live lives of love, harmony and goodness. In time they will bring all their desires within the
law of good.

Here is another method of restoring my soul and
remembering paradise. When I go to our great libraries,
see exhibits of inspiring and beautiful paintings or meet
spiritually developed and outstanding people who have
done great and good works, I go home and remind myself that every man is seeking paradise. And we should
all remind ourselves often that the song of every heart,
the hope of every soul, the motif of every painting, of
every architectural gem on earth, the theme in every
great poem and story, the search of philosophy and of
science are all the same search, the same desire—desire
for perfection. This is a hunger for love. It is a hunger as
old as man which has led him from considering the clods
underfoot to considering the stars overhead. We should
let this remind us that man cannot fail. It should increase our faith in the power of love; should help us to
release our worries and let God's love lead us.

We come to the place where merely living or earning
a very good living is not enough. Finally we learn to
join forces with God for the progressive good of all
other men as well. We no longer ask God to love us and
be on our side to help us build perfection. We go over
to God's side and find that we are entering paradise,

that we ourselves are building it. We overcome our impatience and fears. We work quietly, sure of the outcome.

If we are unhappy about things as they are and truly desire a better way of life we should go to God as little children and *trust Him*. When we truly desire perfection, we will bring our desires, acts and beliefs under God's law. If we will but trust this moving, creating spirit within us it will bring us safely at last face to face with outer reality, God. Then we shall find peace beyond understanding and joy beyond description. We shall get the final answer to our final question.

No matter what you are trying to do, nor by what name you may call it, you are seeking a more perfect life. Let me give you seven wonderful words which if used, will not only set spiritual forces into motion to bring the desires of your heart to you, but will, after their kind, also keep you so constantly aware of the nature of love that you will automatically trust this creative spirit to lead you on and on to higher and higher states of being.

These words are: *I am changing my life through love.*

You must use them with understanding. You must consciously think about what you are doing and why. Here is what they mean and how to use them.

I am serves two purposes. First, it is a statement of being. It tells a truth or fact. It places you in the universe, states that you are an entity, a portion of God. It tells you not only what you are but how much you are. Second, it makes your declaration known unto the minds of all around you by placing it in the Universal Mind. It thus establishes your purpose in the minds of all and in your own free mind as well. It shows you believe in yourself and your powers. It will therefore draw strong aid from others.

Changing reminds you that old ways are passing; new ways are being instituted; affairs are not standing still. Repetition of the word helps to set changes into motion. Change denotes growth taking place. *Changing* impresses upon your mind the fact that it must draw new things and conditions to you relinquishing the old harmful ones. It orders the creative power of the universe to help.

My identifies you and your affairs from other people and their affairs. It reminds you that you are not dependent upon others for success. When you see others all around you failing in their enterprise, when others cry poverty, danger, sickness, bad luck or whatever it may be that you do not want in your life, your affirmation keeps you from wavering in your resolve. You are changing *your* life through love, no matter what others may do. You need not reform the world. Nor can all the world restrain you from your acts. *You* are changing.

Life is the gift of being, of entity, of God, and your share of all that God is. Life as it is invested in man is a free-will power. You may do with it as you desire, multiply it or let it lie dormant. You are not trying to change just a condition of today but your *life,* that selecting, knowing, using, rejoicing and sorrowing part of you. All you have, think and do are being changed for the better. Not only now, today, and for this earthly life, but for all time. For what you agree to on earth is done for you in heaven. We change our very souls for the better when we work with the power which desires to promote the welfare of all men.

Through means by way of, reminds you constantly that something is being employed to accomplish a definite result. It accents the fact that it is possible to do what it is you are attempting to do; that there is a means through which you work, that it is not all up to you alone.

Love here means God at work in your life by your invitation and desire. It means nothing can or will work successfully against you. You can interchange the words God and love saying "I am changing my life through God" and be correct about it.

If you will accept these facts for the truths they are and put them to work in the way outlined by the previous chapters, you will find that you are bringing all your desires, acts and belief under love. You will find that you are not only changing your life for the better, but that you are actually building a private paradise on earth.

People come to me for help who have been using wonderful prayers and affirmations for years with little or no result. The trouble is they have repeated them like parrots, putting neither thought nor emotion into them. It is our feeling about a matter that sets us into action. It is our deep emotion, our unequivocal conviction, born of our understanding, which sets the power of love moving for us. But we still have to accept that love, still must put our faith to work.

So, start to work with those seven words. Get excited about the thing you are trying to accomplish. Feel deeply about your life, your eternal growth, and the perfection you are building, as you work with the words. Remember words are living things and create after their kind. Our feeling gives them tremendous force as we project them out into the ether world around us. When you use those seven words, accept the love offered by God, feel that there is a power which loves you and desires to guide you on to higher states of consciousness. *Trust* it, and it will never fail you. Trust it, and you will throw away your worries. You will lead a life of serenity and sureness meeting with new adventures, new opportunities to grow but never with a real insolvable problem.

Add to your notes:

Before you fall asleep at night, relax, smile, put aside every anxious thought. Think over the many blessings of the day. Thank God for the gift of life, the blessing of living. Say: "God is with me, and I have nothing to fear. God blesses all men and holds them dear. God's world is good. Tomorrow, when I wake I shall know just what to do all day long in order to work for God, myself and my fellowmen. And I am grateful that this is so."

In the morning when you wake, smile, remember who you are and what your possibilities are. Be eager for the day's work knowing that you can get help for the asking. Do not shrink from any struggle, or effort you know you'll have to make that day. Realize that because it is in your life, you will use it for growth. If the problem of the day is a result of a past mistake don't blame God or your fellowmen for it, recognize it for what it is, forgive yourself, learn a lesson from it, vow to do better and start the new day with a light heart, rejoicing to be alive.

Say: "*This is the day the Lord has made. It is a good day and I shall use it fully and well. Today I shall grow nearer to perfection, nearer to all good, nearer to God. And I am grateful that this is so.*"

Then as you go about your duties during the day keep on remembering *you are changing your life through love!*

CHAPTER TWELVE

To Heal, Prosper and Lead the World

As THIS is being written, there is world-wide fear of a Third World War. Guns roar over the Holy Land. Fear and hunger from the Second World War are still stalking the earth. Some of "the authorities" view with alarm the condition of humanity.

In the previous chapters we have been talking about changing our individual lives through learning the law of love and how to live within that law. But now the question arises, what about the world? What can you and I do as lone individuals to maintain our way of life in a world so seemingly hostile to love, so bent on hate, revenge, greed, and exploitation. We must take these festering little worries and attitudes out of our hearts and look at them one by one. Until we do, we shall find that our individual life-changing remains a very temporary affair. Remember that what we think about the world is part of our total attitude which comprises the three steps in changing our lives—desires, actions, beliefs.

So, let's look at our hidden thoughts and fears about the world and our fellowmen in order to learn how to *trust love to heal, prosper and lead the world.*

In our secret hearts we are saying yes, we can change our own lives through love, but until enough other people far and near do likewise, how much good does it really do us? If we are not to use force with our brother, what can we do about those individuals at home who become alcoholics, who are always on relief, in prison, fostering Communism and strikes, crippling legislation, or who indulge in all manner of dishonest and unethical business procedures which make our dollars harder to earn and less secure once earned. How long must we put up with the spiritually illegal acts of others who have no desire and no intention of changing their way of life? How long must we tolerate such people who are either very much determined to change our way to theirs, or else content to remain helpless and harmful burdens to society?

"And what about those abroad?" we ask. If we are not to use force with our brother, can we do nothing to prevent the threatening wars of aggression or retaliation which bleed and impoverish those who want peace and are willing to maintain it? Must we slave to buy bread for the people who blackmail our hearts, for those who refuse to learn how to produce their own or those who are so broken from wars or political enslavement that they cannot. And will our children and grandchildren after us inherit this burden?

Thus we murmur. Now let us look at some truths.

We can't enforce peace with show of guns. Standing armies, it has been proved, ruin a nation's morals and drain its resources. Europe has always had standing armies that always have become marching armies. For generations Germany put her faith in military might. Look at her today and look at what she has done to Europe.

Treaties will not work. Men do what they intend to do regardless of what they say. Desire for war always reduces treaties to mere scraps of paper. Yet wars must cease. Not only because the human race can no longer finance them, but because we now have the atomic bomb. The hope of saving one's own life by killing the enemy first, has gone forever.

If guns will not keep the peace and insure our safety, what then? Money? Many good people believe that money will buy healing, peace and safety for ourselves and that used as a primer, it will start a pump of perpetual prosperity which will enrich all men and permanently relieve others of the burden of helping their neighbors.

Yet money in itself can do nothing. If money could have helped solve the ills of the world surely Christ Jesus would have created and piled up mountains of minted gold in His day. Since He knew enough to produce a gold coin in the mouth of a fish to pay a troublesome tax, He surely could have produced enough gold to have created a new way of life for all men ever after. Or He would have taught the elect how to produce gold, for he announced that His purpose on earth was to help men to a free and more abundant life.

Money of itself is no guarantee of health, happiness or peace of mind. Where there is little happiness and no peace of mind, where hate and desire for revenge dwell, where there is no self-confidence, no brotherly love, no love of God, there ill health and desperation will reside, and all the money in the world cannot stop it. Evil begets evil, after its kind.

It is true that the feeling of financial insecurity and fear of hunger are at the root of many ills. It is also true that greed, selfishness, and refusal to live within the law of love breed fear of insecurity and create the very ills we dread. If fortunes were piled into the hands of most impoverished people at home, abroad and around the world, they still would not be guaranteed peace of mind. *Real help comes from the inside.* The more self-respecting, God-loving and neighbor-loving a man is the less he wants help or charity, from the outside. He wants a way of helping himself and will fight to the death for a way of life which will permit him to help himself. If that way is denied him and charity is offered instead, he is quite likely to bite the hand that feeds him. The man who will accept forever and give never is beyond help. He has refused to multiply himself by love. He has chosen not to be a part of evolution. So in any case money alone often does more harm than good.

It is not men, land, guns or money that is needed to heal, prosper and keep the world at peace. *The thing needed is a knowledge of the nature of things, the Will of God, a knowledge of the law of love and willingness to live within it.*

Neither money nor things but the intangibles of spirit are needed to bless the earth. Given those, the material things will be produced automatically. This production, however, cannot be done on a wholesale basis. Because all men have free will, it remains an individual affair.

Living within the law of love alone will heal, bless and prosper the world. This is the lesson millions at home and around the world must yet learn. Until they do learn it, there will continue to be wars, rumors of wars, famine, pestilence and every manner of evil which results from man's ignorance of truth and his greed, hatreds, fears, aggressions and desires for revenge. As long as a nation or a man lives contrary to the two great commandments of love, they will suffer. It is law. It is the Will of God, the way things are. It is life. Love alone can lead a man to more freedom, greater liberty of mind, body and affairs, a more abundant life on every level. This is something which cannot be legislated. It cannot be poured into the minds of men as we pour water into a trough for thirsty cattle. We cannot force a man to desire good for his neighbor or to love another. We cannot force one man to treat another as a brother. We can but punish him when he badly abuses his property or person. We cannot force—but we *can* teach! We can show him the advantage to himself in treating all men as his brothers.

Teach him? How is he to learn? Through suffering. What hurts, teaches. Through benefits. What pleases, teaches. Through telling, showing. He will learn eventually because it is his nature to learn. Sooner or later all men observe that there is only one safe way to fulfill their desires and that is the way of love.

Eventually love will lead us away from exploiting our neighbors, away from race discriminations, greed, selfishness and all other foolish attempts to get a good by setting an evil into motion. *Without love there can be no hope of earth, no promise of heaven.* With love, the desire to promote the welfare of all men, we can build heaven on earth for all men.

The one outstanding fact in the world today is that we can no longer frighten men into submission. Nations can no longer gobble up land and enslave natives into doing their will for we now have the atomic bomb. Let one nation push another nation too far, and the third nation steps in for love or gain. There is only one way of peace left to the world and that is the way of love. It is the most practical, economical and satisfying way ever discovered not only to keep peace in the heart of the individual, but in the hearts of all men the world over. Let us look now at an example of how it has proved practical in world affairs.

For a long time the Filipinos had been robbed and exploited by Spain with the result that, their country and their minds were undeveloped. The people had revolted time and again because love, or God at work in man, teaches him he has an inborn right to freedom and that he cannot properly grow toward God without exercising that right. Since time began this prerogative of liberty has revolted against the enslavement of man's God-given free will. It is still going on around the world and will eventually unseat every dictator and unveil every religious untruth. The leaders in the Philippines knew these truths. So they continued to revolt.

When the United States of America took over the job of protecting the Filipinos in 1898, she went there with the intention of love. She found the people about 95% illiterate. She sent some twenty-thousand school teachers there in the space of forty-four years and reversed the situation. Today, the people there are only about 5% illiterate. The Americans taught their brown neighbors how to plant, reap, and increase their food supply. They brought in medicine and built hospitals and schools. They truly desired to promote the welfare of these people. That was love at work. Did it pay off? Well, the Filipinos saved their white brothers' lives in World War Two and remained loyal to America and the Allies through bonds of love.

Some of the other great nations of the world have not seen fit to serve their neighbor with love. Just south of the Philippines lie the Dutch East Indies, for three centuries under Dutch control. The people of these Islands are still only about 5% literate.

The pattern of exploitation, domination, and greed rather than love at work, has scarred the face of earth and embittered men's hearts for centuries. We see the unhappy results the world over, today. Surely no one who is familiar with history was surprised to find most of the Oriental Colonials remaining either bitterly neutral or turning traitor to the Allies in World War Two. Exploitation sows hate and a desire for revenge. Love alone begets love. Not only must individuals learn to love or perish but so must nations. The way to keep a mighty Empire from breaking up is not only to put more love to work within the Empire, to promote the welfare of its subjects, but to repeat the pattern of love at work in all its dealings with all peoples the world over.

Men will eventually see the folly of their ways and turn to helping their neighbor instead of exploiting him as the best means of enriching their own pockets and protecting their own lives, *but will they turn to love in time?* How much love is needed and how much is there already at work in the world? How many people already believe in good for all as a way of life? Is it a majority or a minority, and what are the chances of love keeping the peace of the world? Let's look at some facts.

Never before in the history of the world have there been so many people trying to live a life of brotherly love, of good for all men!

Many of these people have come to the Christian way of life not through feelings of religious fervor, love of God, but because they have seen the grim necessity of it as a way of insuring their own lives and fortunes. They have caught a glimpse of Truth, the established principles Jesus was talking about. When they have grown a little higher in moral consciousness, they will continue to live in love as the result of a joy and peace that transcends all definition. In the meantime, we can trust the spirit of love, God, to continue to work in the hearts of men everywhere. Consider the following:

There are some 79,000,000 Christians in the United State alone! One group of them, the Methodists, who number about eight million, operate around the world today solely in labors of love with the honest intent of promoting the welfare of God's plan for the progressive good of all men. They go to release men's minds from ignorance, to help their neighbor find God, to teach him spiritual laws and how to live within them. They take their teachers, schools, medicine and their "show how" with them. They seek to liberate, not to dominate. They seek to build, not to exploit. They take love and find love waiting.

These good Methodists decided on a Crusade for Christ a few years ago and have since been collecting and spending millions of dollars around the world in works of love! They are exchanging beauty for ashes, joy for mourning and praise for bitterness not only in the war-torn countries, but in all countries. They are building schools and churches, helping individuals and groups, telling the story, of Christian living and teaching the law of love.

Add to the efforts of the Methodists, only one denomination, the efforts of countless others and you will get a very heartening picture of love at work. We cannot mention them all here. But we must mention one other, that of the Unity School of Christianity which sends tons of free literature around the world. This reading matter goes to some seventy-seven foreign countries. It is sent free into prisons, institutions of all kinds, schools for the blind and wherever a request is made. The expense of all this is supported by free will offerings, *love money.*

The American Bible Society has been distributing Bibles for 132 years. During the year 1947 this society shipped into Japan a total of 1,547,079 copies of the New Testament plus 747,594 Bible excerpts and 14,190 complete Bibles. To appreciate that love is at work as never before, compare those figures with these: Previous to World War Two the distribution of Scriptures into Japan only averaged between 140,000 and 150,000 per year. That comparison demonstrates the growth of love at work in the hearts of men. Around the world men are hungry for Christ's truth, and Isaiah's prophecy that the government shall "be upon His shoulder" is being fulfilled.

Aside from our long recognized orthodox churches which are at work around the world, there are hundreds of Truth and New Thought movements not so well known to many, with churches and Centers throughout the world. Their one objective is to tell the story of Christ, the fatherhood of God, the brotherhood of man, and the power of love with the intention of helping others to understand and live accordingly. It should give our faith in love a tremendous uplift to know that there are also some three million Truth students in Japan.

If your faith needs further bolstering then be sure to read *Our Roving Bible* by Dr. Lawrence E. Nelson, director of the division of languages and of graduate studies at the University of Redlands, California. You will discover the fact that there are more people reading the Bible today and that more Bibles are being printed than ever before in its history.

But are we in time? Can we persuade those who, for

selfish reasons of their own, will not help to heal and educate the world through love, as a means of helping themselves? *Can God be mocked?* That is the only question. All else is mere repetition.

Long before we were on earth to worry and wonder, love was at work in man, leading him ever toward God. Long after we are gone love will still be at work. Our children and grandchildren are perfectly safe just as long as they, too, trust the spirit of love and choose to work with it. Not all the world of evil put together can truly harm those who work with God. Jesus said, "What is that to thee; follow thou me." We need not worry about those who refuse to work. Jesus warned what the end of those would be. They cannot harm us; they can but harm themselves.

So we come down to our answer: the way to trust the spirit of love to lead, heal and prosper the world is to cast out our own doubts and fears of its ability and intention to do so. There is no better way to do this than to become active in a work of love either locally or around the world. We are working for or against love every time we think, give an opinion, voice a desire, or commit an act. We are working for or against world good every time we listen to our radio or read our newspaper, for when we do, we respond for or against love, the good of the world, and ourselves. The trouble is we forget that we put forces into motion every time we speak, every time we accept an opinion.

We shall not worry about world conditions if we live our lives at home as we should. Let us send our prayers of love out to the world, and then with the confidence of a child, really trust the spirit of love to heal, prosper, guide and help the world. Let us remember that love is alive in the hearts of good men and women around the world. Let us remember that love never fails. Love had the first word when God said, "Let there be." Love shall have the last word as to the fate of man.

If we will tithe our time, our money and our talents, trust and work with love we shall have no real cause for worry. We must work. We must speak out for a better world. We must let our own light shine. Wherever we see desires expressed, deeds done, and beliefs stated which are contrary to the law of love, we must protest with love. And we must know that our lone voice will carry weight. For when we speak up for love, we are representing God. In addition to acting alone, we must join our individual force with the organized forces for good.

Oh yes, love is still in charge regardless of how many strutting dictators with hobnailed boots and blood on their hands are bent on restricting and destroying the rest of the world for their own evil ends. Let them shout, rattle their sabers and stalk the earth. Let them brag and threaten. The spirit of love in the hearts of free men who have found God and who know the power of love, will stop them. Churches and schools are still being built. Books are still being written and bought. Hope is alive. Prayers are answered.

Let us daily remember that there is a spirit of goodness in the very air of the world and in the heart of every man. It is the great infinite spirit of God which is all love. This spirit desires good for all mankind and works earnestly to promote that good. This spirit cannot be killed in the heart of one man by the threats, disinterest or ignorance of another man. God is not mocked. But God *can be refused*. Each man has free will and can kill or nourish the spirit of good within him. Everywhere an increasing number of men are listening to the voice of God. For only one example, on my desk at this moment are sixteen recent letters from Germany all of which bear out this contention. And there are others from around the world, including Japan.

This spirit of goodness has prevailed throughout time. It has always led man forward. It took him out of caves. For generations it has been at work persuading man to stop killing his brother as a means of enriching his own life. We learn as a race, for here and there an individual listens, learns and hastens to point the good way to others. We have almost learned it does not pay to take up arms against our fellowmen. Presently we shall see it does not pay to take up words, laws, or deeds against them. The greatest strides will come when we work on the spiritual plane and see that we must have no *desire* against them.

No desires against our fellowmen! That day is coming. We are learning the full implication of Jesus' words when he said "that whosoever looketh on a woman to lust after her hath committed adultery with her already in his heart."

Once we come to a three-way method of improving life, the physical, mental and spiritual way of promoting our own welfare and the welfare of all men, we can at last be called true sons of God. Before that we are only hopeful and trusting candidates who are children of God like all men, but not yet come of spiritual age.

"But listen! The war drums are already beating!" do I hear you say?

Oh yes, I hear them. But hark now, there is another sound, a rythmic beating that is lower, faster. That is what I am listening to. It is the sound of the human heart beating out a rhythm of love, a song of God alive in man. That is what you too should listen for, my friend.

For love is on the march as never before in the history of the world. It is marching all over the world creating safety, beauty and good everywhere for all men. It is marching twenty-four hours a day. Change your own life through love and you will have joined that army. By changing your own life you help to change the world for the better.

Let us put our trust in God's desire for our welfare, His love and ability to maintain us and the whole universe. Let us live all our waking hours desiring good for all, doing good for all, believing in good for all. Then we cannot hope too much, neither plan nor dare too much. For the one who loves and does good is working with God. And to work with God is to be safe, *forever!*

Printed in the United States
78463LV00003B/88